# DHOW TO DEAL WITH DEPRESSION

## DR. TIMOTHY FOSTER

This book is designed for your personal reading pleasure and profit. It is also designed for group study. A leader's guide with helps and hints for teachers and visual aids (Victor Multiuse Transparency Masters) is available from your local bookstore or from the publisher.

**VICTOR**

**BOOKS** a division of SP Publications, Inc.
WHEATON, ILLINOIS 60187

*Offices also in*
Whitby, Ontario, Canada
Amersham-on-the-Hill, Bucks, England

**AUTHOR'S NOTE:** All people referred to as patients in this book are either composites of several patients' case histories or completely fictitious. No actual patients' case histories have been used. Several actual quotes are used, but never with the actual history or actual identifying information. We do this, of course, to maintain necessary confidentiality.

Recommended Dewey Decimal Classification: 248.4; 152.4
Suggested Subject Headings: CHRISTIAN LIFE: BEHAVIOR; EMOTIONS

Library of Congress Catalog Card Number: 83-51306
ISBN: 0-88207-610-8

VICTOR BOOKS
A division of SP Publications, Inc.
Wheaton, Illinois 60187

# Contents

This book is dedicated to my wife Donna, the most loving person I know. It is surely her support and joy of living that keep me "balanced" enough to spend my days in a profession that focuses so much time on depression and suffering.

Also, thanks to my patients and students who continue to teach me about life, courage, and trust in God.

# Part 1

---

# What Is
# Depression?

# 1

# Introduction

Last week, Mary came into my office for the first time. "I just don't feel well," she began. "All I do is cry. I don't hurt anywhere. There's nothing wrong in my life right now. My mother isn't dying, I'm not dying, my family is healthy. I don't care much, yet I do love my family, so I contradict myself in one breath. I don't have anything to be depressed about. I don't lack anything. I don't have any problems with my children. I get up every morning and say, 'Today I'm going to be better,' but it never works out that way."

Mary was depressed.

Why talk about depression with Christians? Because Christians get depressed. Mary is a fine Christian woman who now has to deal with more than her depression. As a Christian, she has to deal with self-imposed guilt feelings. And some of her Christian friends and family add further guilt by implying that "good" Christians *never* get depressed.

The tendency to spiritualize depression is probably well intended, but it is still unloving, judgmental, and wrong. In fact, I have observed that depression is experienced almost as often by vibrant, mature believers as by those who "lack spirituality." Some people who have never been depressed find that after trusting Christ as Saviour and joining a church they get depressed for the first time in their lives. I'll share more about that particular kind of depression in a later chapter. For now, the point is, depression is real. And it's real for Christians.

Depression can cause loss of job, disruption of relationships, deterioration in confidence, inability to "feel" God's closeness (you might "know" it but you can't "feel" it), physical illness, and yes, even death. It's somber reading, but Christians can't continue to ignore a condition so debilitating.

## The Symptoms of Depression

Feeling sad is but one of several symptoms of depression, though it or any other isolated symptom should cause no immediate concern. However, if three or more of the following symptoms surface, depression is a strong possibility.

•*The blahs.* The first symptom of depression is a loss of emotional feeling, commonly referred to as the blahs. Perhaps you've even said it yourself, "I don't feel particularly bad; I just don't feel particularly good. As a matter of fact, I don't feel much of anything." That's the blahs. We may call it the Monday morning blues, or some other name, but it's a common condition, experienced by almost all of us. The blahs can be caused by physical problems (catching a cold, for example), or by laxness in spiritual nourishment.

But the blahs can also signal an approaching depression. For most of us, most of the time the blahs proceed no further. Our mood merely drops to the blahs and then returns to normal living. Yet we need to be aware that every emotionally caused depression starts with a case of the blahs that hangs on and very gradually deteriorates.

•*Overly self-conscious.* Several years ago, I was moderately depressed for two months, during which time I remember becoming painfully self-conscious. Since then, I've heard this symptom spoken of over and over again. I recall eating lunch at the same table where I had eaten lunch the past four years with my same close friends. Same table, same place but suddenly I didn't know who to look at, I didn't know what to eat next on my plate, I didn't know where to put my hands. I was overly self-conscious.

Another way of expressing this symptom is to say that much of what we do during the day, we do by "automatic pilot." We drive the car, cross our legs, scratch our noses, turn our heads, with virtually no conscious thought or decision involved. When we are depressed, that automatic pilot is often out-of-order. Suddenly, little decisions require conscious thought, and we become self-conscious.

Common sense tells us that there are times and situations when some self-consciousness is normal, such as being in a group where everyone knows what to do except you. But when it is not appropriate to the situation, it may be a symptom of depression.

•*Change in sleep patterns.* Depression is often associated with sleeplessness. There is no doubt of that, but sleep can be disturbed in many ways. Jack says, "I can always tell when I'm getting depressed because I'll wake up about 3 or 4 in the morning. I go to sleep quickly at bedtime, but then I'll be awake and there's no going back to sleep. That's always my first clue that something's not right."

Ruth's sleep pattern is changed by depression too, only hers is quite the opposite. She says, "When I'm depressed, I sleep. I sleep all the time. I can wake up, have breakfast, and take a two-hour nap. I'm tired constantly. And if my husband and I ever argue, I don't fight back. I just take a nap. I know I must be hiding from something, but that's just my way of handling things."

Obviously, sleep disturbances can have causes other than depression, including overeating or too much caffeine. If sleep disturbance is your *only* symptom, don't be alarmed. Recognize, however, that it is *a* symptom of depression.

•*Change in eating patterns.* A marked increase or decrease in appetite can also signal depression. Be aware of extremes such as an extended loss of appetite or constant eating, both telltale signs.

•*Change in crying patterns.* Perhaps you cry regularly and suddenly you're not crying at all. Loss of normal crying pattern is a *strong* indication of depression. Something is holding back the tears; an emotional blockage is interrupting the normal flow of emotions.

Another equally strong indication of depression is the feeling that you need to cry, that tears are always just about an inch below the surface. Of course, constant crying or crying for hour after hour is an obvious warning sign.

•*Loss of confidence.* As the depression builds, there is usually a growing lack of confidence, coupled with a lack of initiative and energy. Loss of confidence can become so intense that you literally cannot function normally.

A woman once told me that she spent an hour standing at one spot in the supermarket, unable to decide whether to buy ready-made rolls or corn muffin mix for her husband's dinner. Finally, she had to call her husband to tell her what to do. It wasn't because of her super-submissive personality—she was depressed.

Many depressed people stop driving, withdraw from social contacts, worry excessively, and may even have to leave their jobs. The loss of self-confidence can reach the point where they stay in bed because that's about all they can handle.

•*Drop in mood.* The final major symptom is the feeling of sadness often associated with depression. While depression often starts with feeling "nothing" or the blahs, the mood doesn't stay neutral very long. Eventually the mood drops and a strange combination of sadness and not caring results.

## Normal or Depressed

Now that we've seen the main symptoms of depression, our minds move to the obvious questions, "What is depression?" and "What causes it?" The answers to these questions are necessary to discover depression's cure. We need to know "what's broken" before we can fix it.

How do you find out what's broken in your television? If you're like me, you shake your head in bewilderment at the insides of a TV and call the repairman. But the reason the repairman can fix your set is that he knows how it is supposed to work. In a school for TV repairmen they study TVs that work. In its essence, repair work of any kind is finding out how the broken thing differs from a working thing and changing what's broken to make it normal again. (By the way, for those of you with a philosophical bent, when I say "normal" functioning I mean "healthy" and not "average.")

## Normal Emotional Functioning

Let's begin our brief look at normal emotional functioning with an even briefer look at the brain and the heart. First, the brain. We know that our brains are awake all the time, even when we're asleep. (I know what you're thinking. Some of you are pretty sure your Uncle Charlie's brain is not awake all the time, and you're positive your teenager has frequent lapses.) But be that as it may, it is the brain that produces dreams while your consciousness sleeps. It is also the brain that keeps your lungs expanding and your heart beating during sleep. It is as though there is a constantly flowing stream of thoughts, directives, and messages that the brain produces.

In much the same way, there is a constantly flowing river of emotions within us. The stream of thoughts flowing in our brains, of course, occurs in our *heads*. For the sake of comparison, imagine that the constantly flowing river of emotions occurs in our *hearts.*

In normal emotional functioning an emotion occurs in the heart, then is sent to the brain for identification, or to use an analogy, for packaging and labeling. The brain responds appropriately, for example, "Aha! I'm feeling embarrassed."

From the labeling and packaging part of our brains the emotion is sent to shipping and delivery where, quite often, the emotion is delivered by *saying aloud* the packaged and labeled *name* of the emotion. As in, "I'm embarrassed."

Obviously we don't talk constantly about the names of our emotions. But if it's a significant emotion, an emotion of any kind of intensity or strength, ideally it comes to our brains where at least we can know it consciously and label it. Then whenever appropriate, or whenever necessary, we speak it. *Because normal emotional functioning is a continual flow of emotions,* we speak an emotion to get it outside of our insides. When our emotion hits the light of day, it begins to dissipate.

From time to time, I may come home from the office in a bad mood. On those days I know ahead of time that I'm going to be critical and easily irritated until I get myself back in tune. In other words, I have an emotion inside me that is either going to come out directly, verbally, and under some kind of control; or it's going to ooze out the cracks in my personality and there's no telling when, where, or how it will erupt. At those times I'm a prime candidate to express my emotions in an unspiritual way.

For the last few years, however, I've practiced a technique that definitely works better for me, and for hundreds of my patients to whom I've been teaching it. This method produces an emotional expression that *is* Christlike and controlled, *is not* irritable or destructive, and *prevents* both emotional explosions and depression. Don't misunderstand, I didn't invent it. I'm just illustrating what I am convinced is normal emotional functioning.

What I now try to do when I come home in a bad mood is simply say, "Family, I have an announcement. Daddy's feeling crabby. It's not your fault. It's mine. I walked in the door this way. So, watch out for me for a little while, and I'll work on it."

Believe it or not, within 5 or 10 minutes of expressing that emotion, it's gone. Not stuffed down inside, but released and able to dissipate and be replaced by the next emotion to occur.

Releasing or delivering an emotion is healthier than storing it inside ourselves. Furthermore, releasing or delivering that emotion in a way that is loving and controlled is more Christlike than either an uncontrolled expression or repressing it altogether.

## Depressed Functioning

Using our analogy of first producing emotions, next labeling them, then packaging and shipping them, what would happen if a particular factory continued to produce a new product (emotion) every 10 minutes, and the shipping department refused to deliver any of them? What if every emotion was stored in the basement?

Soon the basement would be full to overflowing. The conveyor belt could no longer be unloaded because of lack of storage space. Eventually the entire assembly line would be affected.

In a very real way, that is what happens to cause depression.

A depressed person is emotionally obstructed. A logjam of backed-up emotions exists. Something inside us says, "Oh, no! That's going to hurt too much if I feel that!" Or perhaps, "Oh, I'm not allowed to feel that!" Or, "I can't face that!" At that point, it is as though our shipping and delivery department goes on strike. This will *inevitably* cause internal pressure and become the *general* cause for virtually all emotional depression. (We'll spend several chapters looking at *specific* causes.)

You will remember that we said that stage one of depression

is always the blahs. Perhaps you can see now why that is so. We've turned the valve and shut off our emotional pipeline. What then is left for us to feel emotionally? Nothing. That's the blahs.

## Grief
People get depressed because they don't allow themselves to feel or express a primary emotion such as grief.

When I worked at a psychiatric hospital several years ago, I practiced a method called psychodrama. In psychodrama we often dealt with depressed people who were depressed because they were grieving. Actually they grieved internally, but didn't go through the outward grieving process. Many of you have had loved ones who have died, so I think you'll relate to the following story. It's a very typical one.

Mrs. Chaney, a Christian, was about 60 years old when she died suddenly. Her five children came to the house as soon as they could. As it happened, the last to arrive was the oldest sister Roberta, who was always the sibling leader. When she arrived everyone said, "Oh, we're so glad you're here. Now you can make all the arrangements because we just can't. It hurts too much."

So Roberta did what she was used to doing, holding everyone together and making all the arrangements. The rest of the family leaned on her and she prayed and leaned on the Lord, somehow making it through those difficult weeks.

Sadly, however, she didn't feel the sense of loss. She didn't cry; she didn't feel grief. She pushed it down. There was no time to grieve now. She was too busy supporting everyone else. These were, no doubt, good motives. There was no lack of faith and no sin.

About a month later the rest of the family began to pull out of the grieving process and adjust. They missed Mom and cried occasionally, but they gradually ended their grief.

Roberta also operated normally for the next year, even though she didn't grieve. But then just about 18 months after her mother's death, Roberta became very depressed. (Depression of this type usually takes just about 18 months to develop.) She cried almost constantly, couldn't sleep, and started to miss work. Finally, she began to stay in bed all day until her husband took her to a psychiatrist. Roberta's situation is common among depressed people who for one reason or another repress grief. She will be fine, but she'll have to go back and feel the grief she didn't allow herself to feel before.

## Pressure

I wonder how many of you have cooked with a pressure cooker. Imagine a pressure cooker under intense heat, the lid securely fastened, but the pressure release valve stuck. The lid would surely blow off and you'd have spaghetti sauce or beef stew all over the room. Well, just like a defective pressure cooker, a depressed person has a stuck pressure release valve.

If you don't have a pressure release valve, you're going to have a tremendous buildup of pressure inside, resulting in an emotional explosion, implosion, or a breakdown of some kind. Christians operate by exactly the same laws of psychophysics as everyone else. (Psychophysics refers to the regular and predictable ways in which internal emotional pressures and stresses will act and interact within our minds and bodies.) Having your sins forgiven is great, but it doesn't change the laws of psychophysics. God is the One who established those laws in the first place and they apply to everyone.

## Guilt

Depression can also be caused by not feeling guilt. I counseled a pastor several years ago who was very depressed. It didn't take many therapy sessions to find out that he was depressed because he had been caught having an affair with a college-age girl from his church. The girl's father had discovered it, but hadn't yet said anything to the church board. The pastor felt that his job was in jeopardy, and also that he had blown his calling and really let down the Lord, both of which were true.

But rather than feel the guilt and appropriately confess his sin and repent, he shut off the guilt. Initially, of course, he felt nothing, which felt better than feeling guilty. But as soon as he shut off the guilt, the pressure inside built up.

You've probably seen isometric exercises. Push your hands together, keep pushing, and soon you'll feel tension in other parts of your body. This is what happens inside when you need emotional release and you repress it. You begin to use a tremendous amount of energy, and that makes you tired.

When, in the course of counseling, the depressed pastor allowed himself to *feel* the guilt, and also the fear of the consequences from his church and his wife, his depression lifted almost immediately.

In this illustration sin was directly involved in initiating the depression. Yet it wasn't the sin itself, but the repression of guilt and fear that arose from the sin, which made him depressed. It would have been quite possible, and certainly preferable, for him to have confessed and repented of his sin as soon as he committed it rather than repressing (pushing down) those feelings. The sin didn't cause the depression; the repression of the emotion caused the depression.

## Rejection
You can feel depressed because of rejection. Esther loved a man. She loved him deeply. Suddenly she found out he didn't love her back. At that point, rather than feel the rejection and loss of that love she'd privately enjoyed for a long time, and rather than experience the pain of letting that relationship go—Esther got depressed.

Rejection and betrayal really do hurt. And sometimes in an

effort to hold ourselves together—to look strong or more godly —we don't allow ourselves to feel the loss. We don't cry, we don't express anger at having been betrayed, and we become prime candidates for depression.

## Anger

Grief, guilt, and rejection make up, however, only about 20 percent of all depressions. *Not feeling anger* accounts for the other 80 percent.

Remember the pressure cooker illustration mentioned earlier? Depressed people who are depressed because of anger have placed a lid on their rage. Their anger has no place to go, so it hits the lid of the pressure cooker and comes right back down and hits them. Ask anyone who is depressed, "With whom are you angry?" and they'll all give the same answer—"I'm angry with myself"—because that's what they're subjectively experiencing, though it's not objectively true. We as counselors, family, and friends need to help them install that little pressure release valve to let out their emotions, to find out with whom or what they are angry.

We'll deal with treatment in a later chapter, but for now, when you notice that you seem depressed, here's a suggestion. Ask yourself, "With whom am I angry?" Let your mind go blank and look for an answer. You'll probably ignore the first thing that comes to mind, saying, "That's too little. I'm sure it wasn't that." But that probably *was* "it."

You might say, "But it's silly. That's a dumb reason to be angry." Perhaps so. We all have silly reasons to be angry and sometimes our anger is not particularly justified, but it's very real. Sometimes we're angry at people because they won't change. We're angry at people because they won't let us have our way. We're angry with people because they reject us. We're angry with God because He won't do what we want Him to do. We may even get angry at red lights.

## Summary
In each case we've looked at emotions that are manufactured inside of us, often in response to the people and circumstances around us. After the product is manufactured, it exists. You can't ignore it and you can't go on filling your basement forever. When shipping, labeling, and delivery of emotions fail to keep up with their manufacture, there's going to be a logjam, and a lot of internal pressure. The emotional system clogs and depression results.

# 2

# Can Christians Be Depressed?

We come now to the issue of Christian depression. This is a book written by an evangelical with a predominantly evangelical audience, and I think I have already alluded to my conviction in chapter 1. Yes, Christians can be depressed because they have emotions like everyone else; and when emotions are blocked, even for what is thought to be a spiritual reason, depression occurs.

## The Depressed Convert

Over the years I've met several men who closely resemble the following example. Glen was the neighborhood hell-raiser. He was the loudest drunk and the poorest father. Glen was everybody's example of what *not* to be. But miraculously, at age 40, this loud, obnoxious, frequently drunk, poor father, accepted the Lord. His life was miraculously changed.

Now, instead of being everybody's bad example, Glen became everybody's good example. He's told, "Don't get drunk and beat up your kids and scream and swear." He says, "All right. That's good advice. I won't do that." So far, so good.

(Unfortunately, he wasn't given instructions as to how to express his emotions in a Christlike way.)

Glen is obviously a man with very strong natural emotions, but when was the last time you were taught in church how to express your anger or hurt or disappointment in a godly way? The only emotion Glen learned to express was praise.

Consequently, 12 to 18 months after Glen accepted Christ, he became depressed for the first time in his life. He's not depressed because his sins are forgiven. He's depressed because we, as Christians, are pretending we are nonemotional beings and are not giving each other the tools that we need to express ourselves. I hope I'm making that clear. I'm not blaming it on his salvation. I'm blaming it on our pretending that emotions don't exist, or that prayer somehow allows us to violate God's own laws of psychophysics.

## The Exploding Christian

Pretending Christians produce a corollary problem to depression that may not look like depression. Yet it is caused by the same "Christian" tendency to deny and store feelings rather than to confess them. It is the problem of temper or emotional explosions.

Do you remember what happened when you heated a jar of baby food for your child and the lid was screwed on too tightly? You had an explosion!

Perhaps you know someone who is the sweetest guy in the world for two or three months at a time. He expresses nothing negative and is a real Mr. Congeniality, but what's happening is that things are building up, and once every three months, *bang!*

The explosion is caused by the same storing of emotions that causes depression. Christians are particularly susceptible to such outbursts because its only antidote is regular expression, or confession, of emotions, an act some Christians feel is decidedly unspiritual.

To further illustrate the cause of emotional explosions I add still another analogy. Remember the imaginary river of emotions that's constantly flowing in the heart; above the river, lying between the heart and the conscious awareness, is a trap door. Healthy people can open the trap door anytime they want and ask, "What am I feeling?" as they look down to see what emotions are flowing. If an intense emotion occurs, the trap door opens almost automatically to let the steam emerge.

However, the explosive person feels it's wrong to let off steam. He keeps his trap door shut as tightly as possible. What happens to him is as predictable as what happens to a pressure cooker without a steam valve. He explodes.

Christians who do this not only misinterpret Christianity but perpetuate the problem. Let me explain. First, they exploded because they felt it was wrong to express "I'm angry with you." So they didn't express it. They put a lid on it.

Then the pressure builds and builds to the point where they finally can't hold it and the lid blows off. They scream and pound their fists or do something worse. Then they feel guilty and say, "I shouldn't have done that. That was the wrong thing to do. That proves I should never have let out my feelings. I won't ever do that again."

Meanwhile they nail the lid shut again. And what happens when it's too tight? None of the steam gets out, and they guarantee the whole process will be repeated. Some of you know people, perhaps you yourselves, who have been going through this series over and over and over again for years. There's *got* to be a better way, because a temper outburst is certainly a non-controlled, un-Christlike expression of emotion.

King Saul is an excellent example of inability to control emotions. He, no doubt, resented David for several reasons, the most obvious of which was the fact that David, and not Jonathan (Saul's son), was anointed to be the next King of Israel.

Saul apparently tried to control his anger by holding it inside, then invited David to play soothing music because he was so distressed (depressed). But after being with David for a while, Saul just couldn't contain his rage any longer and he exploded. As you know, Saul threw a spear at David and tried to kill him on several occasions, but there is no record that Saul ever sat down and tried to express his feelings to David in an adult, controlled way.

There is a biblical model for communication in Ephesians 4:15: "Speaking the truth in love we are to grow up in all aspects into Him, who is the Head, even Christ." The key phrase is *speaking the truth in love*—an important principle that I don't think we're being taught enough.

Speaking the truth in love is the opposite of speaking only the truth without any love. The truth only is: "Boy, that's an ugly shirt." Or, "I hope you don't get your hair cut that way again. That looks awful." Or, "No, I really didn't want to be with you tonight but my husband told me to come so here I am." That's truth, but it's not Christlike.

Sometimes people give you love without the truth. Love without the truth is: "Oh, what a beautiful dress. Isn't that lovely! It's so flattering. My, oh my, oh my." And they hate the dress, but say what they think is the loving thing. Love without truth isn't honest, and so the person who now thinks she looks beautiful in that dress is going to wear it again and again.

Here's the Ephesians 4:15 solution to the unflattering dress dilemma. Speaking the truth in love is essentially, "I love you. I'm not crazy about the dress." Of course, you need to respond in your own words, mixing your personality with the fruit of the Spirit called gentleness. But giving people the truth in love is biblical, it's psychologically healthy, it communicates clearly, and can definitely prevent both depression and emotional explosion.

Here's another example. Husband is angry when he leaves for

work in the morning because wife forgot to have his blue suit dry-cleaned for his important appointment with the big boss. He decides, "Look, I'm not going to start the day angry. I'm just going to keep my mouth shut." (You'll notice that this is a good motive.) But wife notices that when he's getting ready for work the drawers in the bureau are closing a little louder than normal, and when she says, "Good-bye, Sweetheart" and he can only reply, "Mumble, mumble" she knows something is definitely wrong.

Now suppose during the day husband gets tired of repressing his anger and decides to speak the truth in love. He could come home and say, "Sweetheart, I need to share something with you. This morning I got upset because I reminded you a week ago to have my blue suit dry-cleaned for today's big meeting with my boss and you forgot. I felt all day like there was this wall between us, like we were a million miles apart. I just didn't feel like I could call you from work, so I wanted to tell you as soon as I got home just to make the wall go away. I hate that feeling of distance from you, and I just felt like I needed to share it with you."

That might not have been the greatest speech you ever heard, but it wasn't bad because what he said in essence was, "I'm angry, or I have been, but I don't want to be." I think most of us can take "I was angry about so and so but I don't want to be angry anymore," much easier than we can take silence or not talking about it at all and then exploding.

Many times we say, "Well, I won't talk about it," "Don't make waves," "Avoid struggles, avoid hassles," "Don't hurt feelings," "Peace at any price." We push real feelings down, often under the guise of biblical submission. Perhaps we think ourselves to be kind, or even "peacemakers," but we're not. Repression is spiritually and psychologically unhealthy, and virtually guarantees depression or emotional explosion. How much better to speak the truth in love.

## Long-term vs. Short-term Consequences

The biggest emotional and relational mistake that many Christians make is looking only at short-term consequences of emotional expressions. We look only far enough ahead to see, "If I say this, it could cause pain or suffering, so it must be wrong and I won't say it."

This is a well-motivated decision but it is neither healthy nor spiritual. Suppose friends from church have arrived at your home 30 to 45 minutes late for dinner the last three times they've been invited. You choose to say nothing about this rather than lovingly expressing your anger. But silence is very shortsighted. Your emotional storage room will eventually fill to overflowing and one day you will either overreact and explode (this is genuinely un-Christlike behavior), or you will start to avoid this couple and the relationship will either be injured or die.

Friends with whom we are not honest will certainly never become the kind of close Christian brother and sister that God would have them to be. There is no substitute for sticking out our necks and learning to speak the truth in love. Avoidance is as genuinely un-Christlike as exploding. It destroys relationships instead of protecting them; and in addition, it produces depression.

## Christians in Grief

Grief is another significant category where Christians are perhaps more susceptible to depression than a totally non-religious person. It is all too common to confuse our joy that a loved one is now with Christ in heaven with our troubled sense of loss and emptiness.

Eternity notwithstanding, a widow still has to sleep alone, eat alone, attend parties alone, and go without hearing, "Good night, Sweetheart. I love you." And the hurt doesn't end when she leaves the cemetery.

I must confess I feel angry when I hear a well-meaning, but

misinformed believer tell a widow she shouldn't be upset. Yes, Christ took the sting out of death but the reality of that truth is still future. Man was not designed to die. That only happened because of Satan and the Fall. Death is called "the ultimate insult" to God's Creation and it is clearly Satan's number one weapon. Christ's own death and resurrection ensure that weapon's defeat.

The following is not a composite or fictitious illustration like the others in this book. It is unbelievably true.

I once counseled a 26-year-old pastor's wife who had been terribly depressed for several years. During seminary this young couple's 3½-year-old daughter had tragically died from congenital heart defects, and one of her husband's professors told her, "Every time you cry your little girl cries in heaven, so you shouldn't cry." A seminary professor! The pastor's wife listened to the professor, held in her grief, and of course, became very depressed. Psychotherapy relieved her depression, but years of suffering could have been avoided if those Christians around her had understood more about how emotions work.

Human beings are created with emotions. Christ Himself felt sorrow and when He did, He wept. When He was grieved to the point of death, He told God and His friends. He talked about it. He didn't put up a sign, He didn't advertise, He didn't stop people on the street, but simply shared His feelings with those He knew and trusted. This is very appropriate.

## Christian Pat Answers
We Christians often give a spiritual-sounding answer to a person who's depressed. We'll say, "Pray about it," or "Give it to God," or "Just give up your rights," or "Have a transformed temperament." Pat answers sound good when you read them and work *sometimes* with *some* people in *some* circumstances, but they do *nothing* for the depressed person in his present crisis. Here's why:

Everyone has attitudes (inner feelings or emotions). These attitudes are inevitably confronted by people and circumstances which trigger an emotional reflex or reaction. The process is completed when the emotionally healthy person outwardly expresses the emotion (see figure 2-1).

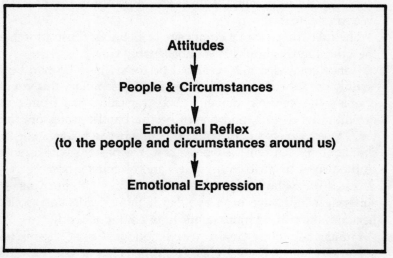

**FIGURE 2-1**

By the time you have an emotional reflex, the attitude of anger, for instance, already exists. The only thing you can do is repress it (store it inside), or get rid of it (deliver it), hopefully in a controlled, Christlike manner.

However, when Christians offer well-meaning pat answers to depressed persons they exhort in vain. When they say, "Give it to God," or "Pray about it," they're really giving the depressed person the implied message, "Don't express what you're feeling. Keep it inside. I don't want to hear about it." When we're upset, none of us wants to hear someone say, "Don't tell me your troubles." Yet to the upset person, "Pray about it" somehow translates into "You should feel guilty for being angry. So, instead of confessing your anger to me, keep it to yourself, pray about it, and get it over with." Or, "I wish you'd pray and shape up and stop being such a miserable sinner." Obviously, we're giving the wrong impression.

There may well be an appropriate time for helping one another purify attitudes. There may well be an appropriate time to say, "Pray about it," "Give it to God," "Have a transformed temperament." But since those comments are aimed at changing attitudes, not at comforting troubled emotions or aiding in their release they should not be used when someone is upset. In other words, *never instruct a person who is in pain.*

The reasons are easy to understand. First, a hurting person won't learn anything while he's in pain. Second, you will probably make him feel worse. And third, by attempting attitude instruction, you might alienate him to the point that he won't listen to you later when he's able and ready to learn.

Pat answers are not only ineffective in helping people, but usually add more guilt and rejection to the emotional pile. You can't redesign a product when it's already in the shipping department. Redesigning of emotional output *is* possible, but what already has been produced must be delivered.

A few more words about attitude. If you see yourself as God sees you, then you face circumstances with an entirely different perspective. It was once thought that the earth was the center of the solar system and that the sun revolved around the earth. Later, when astronomers learned that the sun was the center of the solar system, they could see the rest of the universe more accurately and realized all of their earlier calculations were wrong. Similarly, we need to put the Son of God at the center of our "solar system." We need to see the universe the way He sees it. Only then can we be sure of accurate attitudes, which in turn should positively affect our daily experiences.

We'll have better attitudes *before* we open the sock drawer and find it empty. Because we'll not be self-centered and overly demanding of others, we'll be less likely to respond angrily. However, if anger does rear its ugly head, the best thing to do is release it in a loving, confessing way. *Speak the truth in love.*

# 3

# Depression and Your Body

A paradox exists regarding physical causes of depression as compared to emotional causes. One category is curable and accounts for the vast majority of all depressions (some say over 95 percent). The other category is, in general, much less curable. The causes are much more frightening, much less hopeful, and the percentage of cases is quite small.

The paradox is that the curable category of depression is emotionally caused, yet almost everyone wants to believe that his particular depression is physically caused. Why do people hope for the disease with the poorest prognosis? Two basic reasons surface. First, physical dysfunctions are more socially acceptable; second, physically ill persons tend to be absolved of responsibility in the cause and treatment of their diseases. In other words, it is so hard for us to admit that we are mishandling our emotions that we actually end up hoping that we have a brain tumor, diabetes, or a hormonal imbalance. One woman said to me recently, "Couldn't I just be allergic to broccoli or something?"

## Food, Nutrition, Allergies, and Sugar

Food, nutrition, allergies, and sugar (hypoglycemia) are currently receiving attention as to their possible effect on our emotions. Because much of this research is new and as yet unproven, I'll follow in the footsteps of the Apostle Paul when he said he didn't really know the mind of Christ on a particular issue, but he would give his *own* opinion.

If my sister called and asked me about physical problems affecting her mood, I would say, "Sure, it's possible. If you have reason to believe that your mood is affected by your diet or hormones or something else, or if you're just worried about it, get it checked out. In many cases the exams involve only a blood test, and your peace of mind is worth the investment.

"But," I would add, "if you're concerned enough about your emotions to want to get some tests, while you're at it why not go to see the emotions expert, and get his opinion too."

Often when we have an emotional problem, we ask the body expert and even the spiritual expert, but we avoid asking the emotions expert. I know people who were told they were depressed because of a lack of Vitamin Q, and they stayed on a strict megavitamin program for two years, suffering emotionally all the time, before finally consulting the emotions expert.

People do have allergies. People do get run-down. People do react to different food types. The effect these problems have on emotions is, I believe, not directly on mood but more often on strength, stamina, or energy. For example, if you are chronically congested due to an allergy, you have to work harder just to breathe. Thus you have less energy to cope with normal living and virtually no reserve "troops" to handle emergencies. Under these circumstances, you might be depression-prone.

The conclusion, then, is that many factors can affect your energy level, which in turn can affect your mood or your emotions. The more physically healthy you are, the more energy you have to cope with the emotional aspects of life.

Physical energy is necessary to cope with mental health, but it's not the entire picture. Many depressed people are in perfect physical condition when they start their depression. Physical limitations can and sometimes do affect mood, but a mood problem certainly does not necessarily indicate a physical problem. I emphasize once more: Emotional problems are *usually* the result of mishandled emotions.

## Physical Symptoms of Depression

In chapter 1, I listed major physical symptoms of depression, including changes in appetite and sleep. In this section I want to discuss a different category of physical symptoms, often called psychosomatic symptoms. These are physical symptoms that are caused by emotions rather than by an actual physical dysfunction.

Symptoms in this category range from the everyday, such as tension headache or upset stomach, to the unique, such as emotionally caused seizures. Please understand that these symptoms are not consciously caused. These people are *not faking*. They have *real pain* that they cannot consciously control.

Emotional pressure is a heavy strain: one part of ourselves is trying to express a strong feeling such as hurt or anger, and another part is pushing that emotion back down inside with equal force. If it doesn't lead to an explosion or a drop in mood, that energy-under-pressure has got to go somewhere, and it will often go to our bodies, and usually to the weakest link.

If your weakest link physically is your digestive system, then that's where the emotional symptom is most likely to occur. If you tend to have inflamed joints and connective tissue (arthritis), you probably already know that it worsens when you're under stress.

I've had patients with mildly abnormal EEGs (brain waves) and lower-than-normal seizure thresholds. Under the stress of repressing emotions rather than carefully expressing them, these people may have seizures. The same could be said of people who have migraine headaches, dizzy spells, diarrhea, vomiting, and many other physical symptoms.

Most physical symptoms *can* be emotionally caused, though of course this is not always the case. It is assumed that a patient will get his physical symptom checked out medically before seeing a psychologist. If not, the psychologist will surely require that he do so.

Unfortunately, when the doctor reports the physical tests are normal and asks the patient about stress or suggests a tranquilizer, almost every patient resents it. He says, "That doctor thinks I'm crazy! He thinks it's all in my head. But I'm not making it up. My head really does hurt. He just can't find out the reason!"

But the doctor is not suggesting you are faking anything. And he doesn't think you are crazy. Physicians know that *50 to 80 percent of all visits to the family doctor have an emotional component.*

Another complaint doctors hear is, "But I'm not depressed. My mood is fine." Your mood may be fine, but remember that the emotional energy went to part of your body *instead* of affecting your mood. Generally, a repressed emotion can do only one of four things: (1) it can affect your mood, causing you to be depressed; (2) it can cause neurotic symptoms like phobias or compulsive behavior; (3) it can cause emotional explosion cycles; or (4) it can go to your body. The fourth category, the physical complaint, can still be called depression even though the mood is only obviously affected in the first category. The second and third categories are not commonly called depression, but are a result of the same emotional blockage.

## Physical Treatments for Depression

When we think about treatment for physical depression, our minds go immediately to the use of prescribed medications. We will, of course, discuss these but other physical treatments are also worth mentioning.

Sometimes rather extreme measures are used in rather extreme cases. Most notable is electroconvulsive therapy, often called shock treatments, in which the patient (who is usually hospitalized) goes through a series of controlled seizures caused by electric stimulation. Even though today the entire treatment is done with the patient under anesthesia, this method has generally fallen out of favor and is used rarely, and then only for people with unusual depressions that have hung on year after year and have not responded to any other form of therapy. If you've been depressed for a long time, don't go through the Yellow Pages calling all the psychiatrists, asking if they will give you shock treatments. They probably won't.

A more reasonable physical treatment for depression is to strive for good health. We need all the emotional and physical energy we can get. Using most of our energy to cope with chronic physical distress will leave fewer "troops" to fight emotional battles, causing greater susceptibility to depression or explosion. Therefore, check for allergies (including food allergies) and make sure you are getting the proper amount of sleep, exercise, and nutrition.

Moving to the use of medications to treat depression, perhaps it needn't be mentioned, but we must *not* take medications prescribed for someone else and given to us by a friend or relative. Medications used for emotional problems are potent and can have severe side effects. If taken incorrectly, they can even cause death.

If your physician diagnoses depression, he may prescribe one of three kinds of medication—sleeping pills, tranquilizers, or antidepressants.

Sleeping pills are often prescribed because depression affects one's sleep. In general, sleeping pills are best used only temporarily, during a time of emotional crisis. It's easy to become dependent on them; that is why they are usually prescribed to be taken only as needed, and *almost never* over an extended period of time.

The second category of medication is tranquilizers, which slow down or relax a person. Since most depressed people are already slowed down by their depression, this is not generally the best treatment. A serious, prolonged depression, however, may make a person feel anxious, even panicky, in which case tranquilizers may be prescribed. Some tranquilizers are strongly habit-forming and, as with all medications, should only be taken when necessary and as directed. (Incidentally, tranquilizers may also be given to assist sleeping.)

Antidepressants are the third category of medication, sometimes prescribed to support or lift up the mood so that the depressed individual has the energy to begin working on his problems. Antidepressants work much like a crutch, taking weight off an injured limb to give it time to heal. In most cases a crutch is only used temporarily; the same is true of antidepressants.

The way an antidepressant works is quite different from the way an aspirin or cold capsule works. One tablet does not give you eight hours of relief. Most often, it is necessary to take the medication as prescribed for perhaps as long as two to three weeks before you can expect to feel any improvement. Of course, everyone's body chemistry is different so it's not unusual for five people given exactly the same medication for exactly the same symptom to respond in five different ways.

Who should take antidepressants? The specific answer is between you and your doctor. In general, most depressed people that I counsel get better without medication. (Less than 10 percent of my patients take any form of antidepressant.) Most depressions, as we have said, are caused by mishandling emotions. Learning to label and express our emotions, which can certainly help to change our environment as well as ourselves, is usually the only necessary treatment. There is, however, no reason for anyone to be ashamed to take a prescribed medication.

## The Role of the Physician and the Psychologist

I am often asked, "Do psychologists prescribe medications?" No, psychologists do not. The training of a psychologist includes an undergraduate major in psychology (4 years); masters and doctorate degrees in psychology (3 to 4 years); and, to be licensed for independent practice in the health field, generally 2 years of supervised practice. Thus psychologists spend 8 to 10 years learning about emotions and psychotherapy, yet are taught relatively little about the body itself.

A physician has an undergraduate degree in premed (4 years), a doctorate in medicine (3 to 4 years), plus a year of required supervised practice in general medicine called an internship. Of this time, perhaps 4 to 6 months are spent studying emotions. Following internship, the physician will often complete a residency (2 to 3 years) in which he specializes in his chosen field under supervision. To become a psychiatrist, then, it is normally necessary for the physician to complete 2 to 3 years of supervised practice treating emotional problems.

In summary, the psychologist has more training in emotions and therapy, but doesn't know about broken bones, delivering babies, treating flu, or prescribing medications. A psychiatrist, on the other hand, is well-grounded regarding the body and medications, but may not have as much background in the theory and causes of emotional problems and their treatment. Thus if a person's problem is primarily physical and treatable with medication, the physician/psychiatrist is the logical choice for treatment. If the primary cause and/or treatment of the problem is emotional, the psychologist is the better choice.

# Part 2

## Specific Conflicts That Often Cause Depression

# 4

# Problems with Parents

I find myself reacting negatively to the idea of starting this section of the book by talking about parents because I'm afraid readers will think I'm going to blame everything on mothers and fathers. I can picture the psychiatrist with the goatee saying in his Viennese accent, "Why do you hate your mother?" Well, this chapter is not about hating your mother. Whatever happened yesterday, you can blame on your parents if you must, but today and tomorrow are your own responsibility.

Yet we need to talk about parents because it was during the process of interacting with them that part of our personality may have gotten stuck at a child's level. We need to get "unstuck" before we can find better ways of functioning.

## Successful Parenting

I'm not sure that successful parenting is as difficult or complicated as it's portrayed to be. Perfect parenting is an impossibility, but that's not the same as successful parenting. The primary objective of parenting is to produce an independent adult. Parents don't fail as parents if their children get Ds in

French or algebra. *Parents fail if their children remain children.*

To become a mature adult, a child needs enough confidence to try new things and to think for himself. He must be able to make decisions, even difficult ones, and stick to them. He must be able to postpone immediate gratification in hopes of achieving greater, long-term gratification. He must know himself fairly well, and be relatively pleased with most of who he is.

The parent's goal, then, should *not* be to coerce or manipulate a child into thinking and behaving exactly like the parent. Parents are not supposed to be in the business of creating clones. And parenting is not supposed to be a lifetime career, but a temporary condition. Successful parents are the ones who are constantly trying to work themselves out of a job.

The successful parent is quite strict with young children, having perhaps 50 to 100 rules. But as the children grow older, the number becomes fewer. By the time the son or daughter reaches age 17, he or she is perhaps only six months away from independence with need for only minor restrictions.

## The Permanent Parent

If you accept the concept that the successful parent is one who has strict control in the early years and gradually decreases it until the child is "set free" at about age 18, then you also realize that there are basically two problems that can develop. The first is not to have enough control in the early years, and the second is to never relinquish control.

The controlling type of permanent parent is directly related to a significant number of depressions. Permanent parents are probably well motivated. They want what is best for their children. They just don't realize what is "best" is *not* necessarily conforming to mom's and dad's rules for living. It is "best" to be able to grow up and be an adult.

Permanent parents are great at controlling by guilt, pressure, and manipulation. Their offspring, unwilling or unable to hurt their parents by saying no to them, build up tons of anger, but don't feel free to express it. As we said in earlier chapters, holding down that emotion will eventually produce depression. Many permanent parents are very conservative Christians. We've all seen stories on television about the Jewish mother who controls her children by guilt. Well, the Jewish population has nothing on some Christians, believe me.

I often have my patients keep an emotional diary to help practice releasing their feelings. Here is an excerpt from one of them. (I have changed nothing but the names.)

> My mother was critical of my care of Becky again. Because of cool weather this morning, I had dressed Becky in a sleep-'n-play suit and had packed an undershirt in her diaper bag in case the afternoon was hot. Mother lectured me that the sleep-'n-play suit was too heavy and that if I had planned to change Becky into an undershirt, I should have packed a pair of booties too. Then she warned me that I was not holding Becky securely and that I should not let Becky play with a plastic mixing spoon—she might gag herself. This evening I told Frank how angry I felt about Mom's criticisms.

As you can see, this woman had a very critical, permanent parent. She was 28 years old with a child of her own, but Mother had never stopped mothering.

A 40-year-old woman named Karen, married mother of 3, came to see me some time ago, extremely depressed. Karen's parents were retired Christian workers, who had moved to the town where she lived. That's when the trouble started.

At first, Karen's folks gave her little heart-to-heart lectures about her child-rearing methods. Then they tried to change the way she kept house. They insisted that Karen's family come to dinner every Sunday, but would start to eat without them if they weren't prompt. The situation finally degenerated to the point where her parents felt they needed to give advice on where Karen went with her daughter, or how Karen shopped, cooked, ate, and worshiped. Their influence spread like cancer. They would come to Karen's home and overrule her decisions with her own children.

Where was Karen's husband during all of this? That's a good question. He was there, but didn't want to "cause any trouble," so he kept his mouth shut. Karen desperately needed his protection, but he was so interested in avoiding trouble, he made the situation worse. (This is what the "avoidance" method of problem-solving usually does.)

Here were two permanent parents treating their adult, married daughter as though she were a child. Unless the adult son or daughter insists on being an adult and refuses to submit to permanent parents (or unless there is a spouse willing to protect his mate from this), *there will be trouble*. And that trouble is usually depression. Karen is still receiving therapy, slowly but surely being released from her domineering parents' control.

## The Internal Critical Parent

Parents can also cause problems by being overly critical. Gentle, loving, constructive criticism, particularly in the form of suggestions and especially when it's requested, can be very helpful. But constant correction and disapproval is destructive to the personality in many ways.

Constant criticism makes the one criticized feel like defective merchandise. A child soon feels as though he can do nothing right. He loses confidence in himself which stifles creativity and sense of humor (indeed, whatever is uniquely his own personality becomes suspect). When he senses his God-given instinct to develop as an individual capable of unique contributions, he becomes frightened and confused. A person with a critical parent feels very guilty for the very part of him (we'll call it his "uniqueness") that is essential to becoming whole.

If a person squelches the desire to be different from mom and dad, and that very instinct is the only path out of bondage or permanent parenting, that person is trapped. He develops such a load of false guilt that it is impossible for him to experience God's joy, peace, and freedom until the guilt chains are broken. Of course, as Christians, we just can't call every guilt feeling false, but some may indeed be neurotic. That is a major reason why Christians ought to go to believers for professional help with their emotions. Nonbelievers have a different world view than believers. They therefore have different definitions of right and wrong, of true guilt and false guilt. Remember the Bible's words, "Blessed is the man that walketh not in the counsel of the ungodly" (Ps. 1:1, KJV).

The person who grows up with constant criticism is also hurt because he internalizes the attitude of the parents, causing feelings of guilt and condemnation even when parents are not present. In fact, it can last long after the parents are dead.

## Completing the Cycle

God doesn't want us to live our lives under the bondage of guilt. That is why Christ came to free us. Romans 8:1 (KJV), which reads, "There is therefore now no condemnation to them which are in Christ Jesus," can ring like a Liberty Bell to those who are trapped in a permanent-parent, guilt-oriented relationship.

To break the trap and complete the growing-up cycle (i.e., become adults) we need to acknowledge that God doesn't want us to be carbon copies of our parents. We *are* allowed to make different life choices than they make. We also need to acknowledge that we are of more use to God as a whole person —as an adult—than as a trapped, guilty, fearful person, stuck on a level of emotional childhood. And finally we need to acknowledge that it is quite possible to feel guilty without being guilty.

The next step toward wholeness—and often the most difficult one—is to acknowledge anger toward parents. Anger is a child's built-in, natural reflex when parents won't let him grow up. How that anger is expressed can be right or wrong, but even if you take the position that all anger is sinful, the Bible still tells us to confess our faults, not to hide them within us (James 5:16). Anger must be acknowledged and expressed in as Christlike a way as possible. Holding it in will cause depression.

Problems will develop when grown children don't learn to pull away from their parents, when they fail to come out from under their parents' shadow to become individual adults in their own right. The following is another excerpt from the diary of the patient quoted earlier in the chapter.

> Although I thought I was quite independent, I realize now that many of my decisions are based on the desires of my parents. I am resolved to break free from them. If Frank agrees, no longer will we ruin our holidays by trying to visit both sets of parents and by eating two holiday meals. Our decision of where we worship will not be based on family ties, but where our spiritual needs are met.
>
> No longer am I going to be influenced by the old guilt game. My parents' frequent minor ailments will not change Frank's and my plans for outings, projects, or vacations. This resolve gave me an exhilarating feeling of freedom.

Psychologists sometimes call it a "parentectomy" when inflamed parents are removed for the health and happiness of the patient. But total cutoff is rarely necessary. Parents can usually be forced to back off from controlling their adult children when the alternative is losing contact with them altogether.

It's often hard for adults to realize that their parents need them more than they need their parents. Obviously, it's quite a role change from childhood days. Overprotective, permanent parents are, in fact, the parents with the most need for involvement with their children, and if their children know this, they can boldly set up new rules and guidelines.

Many depressed people react, "Oh, I couldn't say or do anything that would hurt my parents!"

Well, that's probably good motivation, but it's also short-sighted. You see, parents aren't really happy in their permanent role. Not only do they keep their children from growing up, but the children, by failing to pull away, keep their parents from attaining the next stage of life with, hopefully, fewer responsibilities. In other words, the children are helping to keep the parents from becoming successful.

Do you want to make your parents happy? Then make them successful parents by being independent. Don't expect them to take responsibility for your life and problems, and don't let them. Saying no is sometimes the only way to preserve a relationship.

A woman once came to me whose mother had moved into her house "temporarily" after Dad died. After "temporary" had lasted 10 months, the woman was significantly depressed, short-tempered with her husband and children, and virtually avoided speaking to Mother altogether.

Mother, meanwhile, had found a new meaning to her life after becoming a widow. Or rather, Mother rediscovered an old meaning to her life. Mother filled the void left by husband by mothering her adult daughter.

After a few counseling sessions my patient told her mother to move out within two weeks. Of course, there were tears and hurt looks, but Mother was still healthy, able to work and have her own friends, and when forced to, she adjusted quite nicely to widowhood and life as a senior adult. And the beauty is, after she had a life of her own, Mother was able to once again be a friend to her adult daughter and they actually enjoyed each other. Plus, of course, the depression lifted almost overnight. It moved out when the permanent parent did.

# 5

# Childhood Maps

As we continue to look at specific depression-causing conflicts, we come now to a discussion of childhood maps, which to some degree affect everyone.

## What Is a Map?

A map is a guide that tells us what to expect in a certain territory. If you live in a small town you don't often need to refer to a map, but if you live in a city with a rather complex street system you might depend on a map more often.

We don't all need road maps, but we all use psychological maps to help us sort out the incredibly complex system of relationships, behaviors, and emotions in which we find ourselves. We've all heard of culture shock. That occurs when we try to find our way around a new place with our hometown psychological and cultural map. As you can imagine, the experience is a lot like trying to find your way around Atlanta with a map of Boston. Using an inaccurate map can get you more lost than starting out with no map at all. At least with no map, you'd probably ask for help.

What if you are driving in Dallas with a 25-year-old map of the city? Some things would be the same, but much would be different. You would end up making many wrong turns and little progress.

When children enter the world, they invariably struggle with the complex rules for relating, behaving, and expressing themselves. One way that a child tries to cope with this situation is to make mental maps that give him guidelines to follow. The maps are based on his childhood perceptions and guesses about what works and what does not work in his environment.

As you might guess, while some childhood perceptions are amazingly accurate, others are really off the wall. In still other cases, some of the child's perceptions might be accurate for a time, but the rules themselves eventually change. Rules are different for a 30-year-old than they are for a 3-year-old.

Many of us live our entire adult lives basing many of our decisions as well as emotional and relational behaviors on outdated and inaccurate maps of the complex psychological world. Therefore, we often become lost, and frequently depressed.

This book will have been worth your investment if only you become aware of the half dozen sentences you say to yourself about the world, sentences which then serve to guide your behavior. Then, evaluate each of your "guidelines for living" to see if they are accurate perceptions of the world and truth.

## Never Hurt Anyone
One of the more common childhood map rules is, "Never hurt anyone." This is a statement that has a certain ring of truth to it, and its simplicity, universality, and morality strongly appeal to children.

Is "never hurt anyone" a reasonable guideline for an adult to use to control his behavior? No, even the slightest evaluation will reveal this to be woefully inadequate. What if a surgeon used this map to guide him through his day of surgery and pain-filled patients? Imagine him saying, "I am sorry, Mrs. Jones. We could remove your husband's cancerous tumor and he would live. But the surgery would hurt your husband and since I never inflict pain, he will just have to take his chances with the tumor." It's ridiculous, isn't it?

We've all heard parents say, "I know I should discipline him but I just can't bring myself to hurt him." You can see right through those parents, can't you? They are more concerned with themselves and their own feelings than with the child's welfare. Like the reluctant surgeon, they are selfish. It seems far safer and easier to take the "never hurt anyone" approach to life because it appears to protect us from risks. The consequences, however, are not easy or pleasant.

What about the engaged young woman who says to her mother, "I know now that I really don't love Jim, but I don't want to hurt him. Should I marry him?" If you were her parent, I know you would say, "Look, Jill, you either hurt him a little now and he recovers, or you hurt him a lot later and he may never recover."

As adults we often think, "I really feel upset with her but I don't want to hurt her so I'll keep my feelings to myself." Yet we fail to realize that every unexpressed negative emotion becomes a brick in the wall between two persons. If you add enough bricks, the wall eventually becomes so high that you can no longer feel love toward that person. The love cannot penetrate the wall.

Bob and Beth had very strong feelings for each other when they were married. But when I met them in my counseling practice it seemed there was nothing but coldness. In this case, both of them believed in "never hurt anyone," so they held in most of their feelings. Over the years they had repressed such a load of frustration, hurt, anger, and disappointment, that they had constructed an emotional Great Wall of China between them. They got an A for motivation (they meant well), but an F for communication. How often relationships, especially marriages, are destroyed by this lethal combination!

The Bible certainly doesn't teach "never hurt anyone." On the contrary, we are told in John 15 that if we are not bearing fruit we will be "cut off" and if we are bearing fruit we will be "pruned" so we can bear more fruit. Both being cut off and being pruned are painful. But God knows that pain and growth are often associated (see also Heb. 12:5-12 and 1 Peter 1:6-7). Unfortunately, many well-meaning people keep their loved ones from growing because they work so hard at never hurting anyone.

The contrasting biblical truth to "never hurt anyone" is found in Ephesians 4:15, which exhorts us to speak the truth in love. We do need to be concerned about how we speak the truth, but we also need to be truthful.

## Everyone Must Like Me

Another popular childhood map of the world is, "Everyone must like me." While almost no one would consciously agree with this map, quite a few of us say it to ourselves unconsciously.

Carolyn is a young woman with many friends. She has the gift of hospitality and a ready smile. She is also a gifted pianist, former beauty queen, wife of a successful inventor, and mother of three beautiful daughters. Looking at Carolyn and her fine Christian family, many people would tend to think that Carolyn has it all. But she doesn't.

Because of her material comforts and personal qualities, some women in the church resent her. So Carolyn puts herself through unnecessary suffering trying to win over those few jealous women. She says, "What did I do to make them feel this way about me?" And "How can I get them to like me?" She assumes that if anyone doesn't like her, it must be her fault. Carolyn is following a childhood map that needs revision.

When I counsel people who follow this map, I like to tell them about a fact of life I call "the Albertson's Factor." (Albertson's is the name of a supermarket chain in Florida.) If you would go down the street to Albertson's and allow the first 10 people who walk out the door a half hour each to get acquainted with you, you would find some interesting results.

One of the 10 people would really like you and want to be your friend. One of the 10 would moderately like you. One would strongly dislike you. One would moderately dislike you. And the 6 people in the middle could be swayed one way or the other based on your looks, personality, career, etc.

If you then went across the street to another supermarket you would find exactly the same breakdown. One would truly like you. One would definitely not like you. Some you could sway either way.

Life is much more relaxed when you remember the Albertson's Factor. You could buy a new Corvette and give it to the 1 out of 10 who dislikes you and he would take the Corvette and drive away saying, "What a stupid thing for him to do," and he would *still not like you.*

If we go to a party and there are 30 people there, what do most of us do if we find that 1 out of the 30 strongly dislikes us? We tend to spend the whole night playing up to the only person there who isn't a potential friend, either by trying to win him over, or avoiding him, or worrying about him. And we ignore the 29 potential friends. It's not very adult, is it? This behavior is based on the childhood map, "Everyone must like me."

The same principle applies to pastors. If Pastor Smith has a congregation of 100 people, he can be almost sure that 10 people in the congregation will love him no matter what he does. (And he should, therefore, not let the first 10 compliments he hears go to his head.)

On the other hand, 10 of those 100 parishioners are going to be unhappy with him no matter how hard he tries. He, therefore, does not need to waste any time worrying about the first 10 complaints he hears. If only 10 percent of the congregation is unhappy with him, he's doing about average. If that figure rises to about 30 percent he might want to sit up and take notice, but it is neurotic, childish, and crippling to get upset about not having 100 percent approval.

Let's think of other applications of this truth. If there are 10 homes on your street, you have the potential of being very close with 1 of the 10 families. At least 1 of the 10 families won't like you, and it's realistic to assume they'll influence one other family to feel likewise. So if you have varying degrees of cordiality and friendship with 8 out of 10, you get an A+. In the friendship game, 80 percent is a very high A. As children, we got accustomed to aiming for 100 percent. That was fine for spelling and arithmetic but it doesn't work that way with relationships, and trying to force it to work is to try to conform the world to a childhood map, the end result of which is constant disappointment and frustration.

I can almost hear the howls of horror from some saints over my contention that in the body of Christ, as well as in the rest of the world, at least 10 to 20 percent of the people you meet won't want to be your friend. "But Christians are different," they are saying. Well, OK, Christians do have the potential of acting more Christlike, but every Christian I've ever met has also been human and humans have an old nature, as well as human feelings, human emotional needs, and emotional reflexes. Let's not forget that the church is not a club for saints; it's a hospital for sinners.

Some people are teaching that any Christian can and should be able to be best friends and wide open emotionally with any other Christian. I disagree. Surely, Christians ought to be able to get along and treat each other with love and respect, that is true. But "acting in a Christlike manner" is not the same thing as being best friends with everyone.

What about the biblical basis of my contention? The best illustration I know is Christ's own relationships. He had 12 disciples. Out of these, one was called "the beloved" (John), and one participated in Jesus' murder (Judas).

But there were even more levels than that. Though John was Christ's closest friend, Peter and James ranked with him on a clearly different level, a closer level, than the rest of the Twelve. There are several examples (including the Mount of Transfiguration and Gethsemane) where Jesus left the rest in one spot and took these 3 further into a situation. So we have 1 (close friend), 3 (special attention), 12 (selected apostles), but even this number expands. In Luke 10, Christ sent out 70 disciples 2-by-2. There may have also been a group of 500 followers who were called Christ's disciples. And on the outer layer remember that Jesus said that He spoke to the masses in parables so that they would *not* understand what He was talking about. Jesus did not reveal everything about Himself to everyone He met. Jesus knew very well that the more He revealed of His real self the less popular He would be in some circles and the more popular He would be in others.

Everyone is not and will not be your friend. Everyone will not like you. To expect that of them and yourself is to be constantly frustrated and disappointed, and depression is likely.

## Avoid Conflict

A young husband I know noticed during psychotherapy that he was angry much of the day. He discovered that he was angry at everything that kept him from being at home, sitting in a particular chair with his feet up doing nothing. He resented taking out the garbage, getting the car fixed, going to work, mowing the grass, almost everything.

He realized that what he wanted out of life was just to be allowed to sit in that chair and not move. He did not want to be responsible for things. Now he *was* responsible, because he always did what was required of him. It's just that he also hated it.

Of course, as he realized this consciously, he was not at all pleased with his subconscious approach to life and he changed it. But initially, his idea of the perfect life was to just sit. Here was a man who was building his life around the childhood map of avoiding conflict.

Perhaps the way this trait shows up most often in adults is in avoiding arguments. People give in, back off, and swallow their emotions because they don't want to risk conflict. Yet this reasoning is childish because avoiding problems in the short run only means facing bigger problems in the long run.

One of the better definitions of maturity is the ability to postpone immediate gratification in the hopes of greater long-term gratification. But the conflict-avoider is settling for short-term gratification rather than problem-solving. He's pushing down and ignoring his problems, the consequences of which are a clogged emotional system and eventual depression.

Amazingly, most of us would never think of using avoidance as a problem-solving technique at work—it's poor management. But many people who are successful problem solvers at work become problem avoiders as soon as they walk in the front door at home.

So we have wives who have been unhappy at home for years but have never said so because they wanted to avoid conflict. They've stored volumes of discontent and hurt and anger, and it has eventually affected their moods, attitudes, and behavior. They started out innocently wanting to avoid conflict and ended up hurting or destroying their marriages.

Many husbands have spent years practicing how to pacify their upset wives, though their goal may not be clear to them. These men are not trying to solve a problem in an argument with their spouses; rather, they're trying to avoid solving one.

Many problems require only a little attention and they go

away. We've all seen the young child who falls down outside and runs inside crying, seeking comfort. If the parent will give a kiss and an "I'm sorry you got hurt," the child is satisfied, his need has been met, and he goes back out to play. But an impatient parent who says, "Don't cry, you're not hurt. Stop being a baby!" produces a child who is likely to whine all afternoon. In this example, 30 seconds worth of listening and affection, 30 seconds worth of need-meeting or problem-solving can prevent a whole afternoon of stress. We need to grow up and put our energies into problem-solving, not problem-avoiding.

## Growing Up

I know some people are thinking, "Yes, I do have some childhood maps. Now what do I do with them?" I would like to be able to give three magic words to instant maturity, but I can't. (Perhaps that's my own unrealistic expectation.) Growing up is a process. It doesn't happen overnight.

Yet childhood maps can, in time and by God's grace, be put on the shelf forever. First, you must become an observer of yourself. Awareness of a problem's existence is always step one to its solution. Try to identify what sentences you say to yourself about the nature of the world and how to get along in it. If you can identify these sentences, then evaluate them. Ask yourself: Is this guideline for living really accurate? Is it reasonable? Is it biblical? Is it working?

I have consistently noted that when someone has his hand on God's truth and is applying it appropriately, it works. If your method of problem-solving isn't working, maybe it isn't the right method. God's principles work.

Finally, after pinpointing childish statements, try to establish new guidelines that are accurate, adult, reasonable, and biblical. If we will say the same things about ourselves, about each other, and about the world as God does, then we will see things more clearly and with less childhood distortion.

# 6

# Conflicts between Your Insides and Your Outsides

Cathy was a successful career woman before she married. At age 32 she was branch manager of a bank. At 33, Cathy met the man she felt she had been waiting for all of her life, and was married later that year.

The marriage went very well and at age 35 Cathy became pregnant. To say she was overjoyed is putting it mildly. Cathy was always outgoing and witty, but her pregnancy came as close to a hilarious pregnancy as you will ever see.

She was prepared for the baby, happily married, personally fulfilled, and had experienced all the career awards she wanted. She left her job satisfied she had given it her best, and now she wanted to give mothering her full attention, a task she likewise expected to enjoy.

About 18 months later, I met Cathy in my office. She was profoundly depressed and, frankly, in one of the most resistant depressions I had ever seen. We finally pieced together that she was depressed because of an intense conflict between her insides and her outsides.

This category of depression is not so much caused by a failure to express anger or to feel grief, as we have seen earlier, but rather, is caused by having one personality on the inside and another on the outside. The inside personality can't get out and internal pressure builds up, causing depression.

## The Perfect Mother

From all indications, Cathy was the perfect mother. She had read all the books and taken each one seriously. She spent quality time with her child. She said the right things to him in the right tone of voice. Cathy did all the right things . . . but she *hated* mothering. She hadn't expected to, but she did. She was bored, lonely, and sometimes on the inside she wanted to scream and throw a fit. But she never did.

It may be that if Cathy had been blessed with a passive, pleasant little girl instead of an intensely active, strong-willed little boy, she would have reacted differently, but I'm not at all sure that she would have. Mothering and Cathy just didn't seem to get along. Not that she ever used that as an excuse. Her behavior was always appropriate. It was her insides that were unhappy, and a continuing difference between what she felt inside and what she did externally caused her depression.

## The Sloppy Perfectionist

Another woman whom I counseled seemed almost the flip side of Cathy. If Cathy was perfect outside and miserable inside, Lisa was perfect inside and miserable outside. At least she was like that at home.

There was an incredible split in Lisa's personality. Oh, not the kind of split personality you see in the movies. Lisa's split was this. At work, where she was a bookkeeper, she was a perfectionist to the 10th power. But as a homemaker she was a failure. In her desk drawer at work all the pencils faced the same way and on top of her desk nothing was out of place when she left. I heard that her co-workers used to amuse themselves by moving or changing one small detail on her desk and then time how many seconds it would take her to find and fix the erring paper clip. She was obviously an excellent bookkeeper, and at work she was in total control of her job and her work space.

You wouldn't believe what her house looked like. There were stacks of magazines and books three and four feet high in the living room and throughout the house. The trash, the savable stuff, and the articles of daily living were literally piled everywhere. The house was like an 80-year-old hermit's who died and authorities have to follow tunnels to find the body. And every day Lisa's house got worse.

How could it happen? Well, Lisa was a perfectionist. She had extraordinarily high standards and would settle for nothing less. At work she was in control. She could meet those standards. But Lisa had a very laid-back (if not laid-down) husband and two teenaged sons over whom she had no control. The home was not her exclusive domain, could not be kept the way she wanted it, and she couldn't lower her standards and settle for a passably straightened-up, but lived-in house. So she ended up not keeping house at all, and of course, she got very depressed because her insides (perfect neatness and order) and her outsides (super sloppy) couldn't line up.

## The Plastic Personality

Anytime we habitually put a mask on the outside of our real selves we are susceptible to role-conflict depression. Of course, it's not always as severe as the two examples given so far, though both Cathy and Lisa were helped through therapy.

Some time ago I went to the door and there stood a well-dressed young man about 20 years old, short blond hair, no sideburns at all. But in spite of his rather conservative appearance, he was literally bouncing up and down on my doorstep, with vacuum cleaner in hand. Yes, it was that dreaded creature, the door-to-door vacuum cleaner salesman. As I watched in amazement he launched into his memorized routine, "Hello, Sir or Madam, I represent the Handy Dandy Home Maintenance Unit Company of Walla Walla, Washington. . . ." He spoke with incredible speed, and with a singsong quality in his voice that you would expect from a disc jockey on a teeny-bopper radio station, and he did it all while bouncing.

He was an obviously conservative fellow giving an obviously memorized and coached delivery of his speech. The discrepancy between what he was and what he was trying to be made me feel strangely uncomfortable. You know the feeling. I was interested, but not surprised, to hear a few weeks later from a relative that the young man was experiencing emotional stress.

Let's imagine for a moment that there are portholes on the inside of you, in your personality, and more portholes on the outside of you, in your observable behavior. These portholes need to line up, one directly inside the other, to see out. Psychologists call this transparency, and it is necessary to emotional health. The less your insides and your outsides line up, the harder it is to see out (or in) and the likelier is depression.

## Love Conflicts

The person in love can often experience conflict between inner emotions and outer actions. We have all heard of the phrase "unrequited love." When you really care for someone and you can't show it or that caring isn't reciprocated, depression can result.

I've also seen depression occur where persons pretend to be in love when they are really not. They would perhaps like to be in love, or they feel that they should be in love, or they feel somehow obligated or pressured to be in love, or maybe they used to feel love and they don't now. Pretending to love when you don't care is definitely more trouble than it's worth. And it definitely leads to depression.

I hasten to add a clarifying disclaimer about not pretending to love. The previous paragraph could easily be taken out of context and used as an excuse to leave a marriage. It is not intended to be an excuse at all, and refers only to people who are unmarried. They need to be honest, without pretense. Married people need to do likewise, but for a married person, love involves a decision and a commitment and it is, frankly, a different kind of love than most single people experience. (We'll talk more about love and depression in a later chapter.)

I know a man who got depressed because when he fell in love he violated a part of his own personality. He is an adventuresome, active individual, the kind who skydives, climbs mountains, and races motorcycles.

When he fell in love, he unfortunately took too literally the phrase about "getting serious in a relationship." He spent all his time with his girlfriend, and almost all of that in heavy discussions with her. When he stopped letting out the playful, adventuresome part of his personality, he became depressed a few months later. Not only that, but when he stopped being the man she fell in love with, her feelings waned.

## Living Someone Else's Personality
People, especially Christians, are often under pressure to act certain ways. I know of a woman who is a tall, striking blonde, the type often described as statuesque.

Unfortunately, her parents somewhere got the idea that Christians are not supposed to attract attention or be outstanding. Here was a person with a 1,000-watt lightbulb personality and physique and her parents spent her entire childhood teaching her to not stand out in a crowd. (She's almost a six-footer.)

They kept trying to dim her wattage so she wouldn't shine so brightly. Sadly, she grew up believing them and yet her intelligence, quick wit, and looks are hard for her to hide. Whenever she would sparkle for a moment, she would feel guilty.

Self-doubt would overwhelm her and she would be depressed.

God's Word clearly says that there are many different parts of His body, and that some are going to be more visible than others. To change metaphors, God made both diamonds and granite and it doesn't make any sense to cover all the diamonds with mud so that they don't sparkle. This woman, then, was depressed because she had put an artificial veneer of the personality her parents preferred over her own God-given, natural-grained beauty.

The shy child who is born into a family of entertainers or pastors may have exactly the same problem, artificially trying to be something that he can never comfortably be. It often produces depression.

## Christian Behaviors, but Un-Christlike Attitudes

I once counseled a teenager who came from a strong Christian family, and who himself had a solid commitment to Christ. He was a high school senior and most of his friends were having their first sexual experiences. As a Christian he knew what was right, and he was outwardly obedient. But on the inside, he really wanted the same experiences and it made him depressed.

What should you do when the outside standard is right and the inside desire is wrong? First, you need to acknowledge the inside desire or feeling. If you don't acknowledge what is there, you can't fix it. The Bible clearly says we are to confess our faults and not deny them (James 5:16; 1 John 1:9).

In the teenaged boy's case, his behavior obviously should not be changed to conform with his inward desires. But how can his inward desires be changed?

Impulses can be controlled to a great extent by controlling input and environment. Computer operators have a saying, "Garbage in—garbage out," and that is the problem in many situations. I found that this teenager had an afternoon delivery job and spent almost four hours every weekday in his car listening to suggestive pop music. With that kind of input, it's not surprising that his output (his desires) was exactly the same. Choice of friends, TV viewing habits, or off-color reading material might have produced a similar result.

Sometimes we have to change the outsides to end the conflict, as when the Apostle Paul counseled Timothy to "flee from youthful lusts" (2 Tim. 2:22). Sometimes we have to change the insides to conform to God's Word—in other words, develop a mature Christian thought life as Paul advocates in Philippians 4:8. It's not necessary to change our personality, only the sinful impulses. Sinful impulses and personality are not the same.

## Christian Cover-ups
I'm not sure that there's any group more prone to the problem of accepting outside appearance rather than changing what's inside than Christians.

Pretense began immediately after the Fall. Adam and Eve's first act after becoming sinners was to cover up what they really looked like. They were ashamed of their real selves. Their son Cain pretended that he really didn't know what had happened to Abel when he said, "Am I my brother's keeper?" And the cover-ups have continued to the present day.

Perhaps the best scriptural example of an artificial facade to hide inner reality occurs in Exodus 34:29-35 and is referred to again in 2 Corinthians 3:7, 13. It is the veil that Moses wore when he came down from the covenant ratification with God on Mount Sinai.

We read in 2 Corinthians 3:13 that Moses put on the veil so that the people would not see "the *end* of what was fading away." What was fading? The glory that came from being close to God. So Moses settled for the veil, which made it look like he was still as close to God as he had been.

As believers, we hardly pass a day without settling for the *appearance* of spirituality rather than the real thing. The Sunday-morning smile, put on immediately after an unloving car ride to church, is perhaps only the most obvious example. We need to accept and enjoy the fact that we are forgiven sinners, without worrying about how spiritual we appear. For as we have already seen in this chapter, pretense is not only a spiritual problem, but a psychological problem as well.

## Violating Standards

Conflicts between our insides and outsides also frequently develop when we believe one thing to be true and may even be teaching or preaching it, but our lifestyle violates that standard.

The pastor who is having an affair and continuing to preach is a man with a 100-megaton emotional blockbuster about to explode. The depression is almost violent in its sudden attack.

Perhaps the sexual example is too obvious. Every Christian has his own particular weakness where he continues to struggle and fail. For one believer, it is frequent bouts with loss of temper; for another, it is the inability to handle money wisely. But when we continue to violate what we know God wants and what we believe, depression is inevitable. It may not be debilitating, but it can cause Christians to limp along fighting a nagging anxiety and often not even knowing that it is there.

## The War Within You

When your insides and outsides struggle, remember these helpful steps: (1) *Try to resolve the conflict.* It is destructive to have your insides and outsides at war; a house divided against itself cannot stand. (2) *Be honest with yourself.* Don't rationalize the situation. By far, most of the lies we tell are to ourselves. (3) *Be biblical.* If one part of you is clearly in violation of God's Word, obviously that's the part that needs to be changed. But be aware that to change that part of you, you *must* confess your sin to the Father, and you may have to confess or express it verbally to someone else as well. (4) *Be yourself.* Don't be pressured by other people's ideas of what or who you should be. Husbands (and wives), remember that it was who you were when you were dating that your spouse fell in love with and decided to marry. If she succeeded in changing you from the person she fell in love with to her ideal, she might also stop loving you. (5) *It is OK to change certain behavior but don't try to change your personality.* If you are a quiet person, great—enjoy it. You'll never be a stand-up comedian, so don't try to be. Just enjoy being the person God made without artificial flavoring or veneers. If you are a fun-loving person, enjoy that. Don't let the world tell you to be more serious about life. I'm not giving you permission to be irresponsible, merely permission to be who God made you (if you need that).

# 7

# Discontent and Despair

"O God," he begged, "I'd be better off dead. Take my life."

What miserable condition was this man suffering? Was he slowly dying of cancer? Was he totally paralyzed? No, he was depressed. And you might recognize his name—Jonah.

In the Book of Jonah, we have an explicit example supporting the truth that anger is often involved with depression. Jonah disagreed with God's plan to hold an evangelistic campaign in Nineveh and became even more upset when the city miraculously repented. Chapter 4, verses 1 and 2 (NIV) begin the prophet's lament: "But Jonah was greatly displeased and became angry. He prayed to the Lord, 'O Lord, is this not what I said when I was still at home?' " (In modern English, "I told You this would happen!") Following on the heels of this outburst the prophet begs in verse 3, "Take away my life." In verse 9 he pouts, "I am angry enough to die."

Yet God didn't yell at Jonah or reject him or call him names. Instead He helped Jonah see that if it was natural for Jonah to be concerned about a loss of shelter (a vine that withered [v. 7]), it was also natural for God to be concerned with the things that mattered to Him (namely, the 600,000 people living in Nineveh).

## "The World Is Being Poorly Run"

God helped Jonah see the source of his anger and discontent. If depression is often rooted in anger, then we, like Jonah, need to see that anger often arises from the opinion that "the world is being poorly run." In other words, "God, I don't like Your plan at all."

The "submission to God's plan" issue is often linked with depression, partly because we usually don't tell God we're angry with Him. We may think it's unspiritual to be so open with Him about our negative feelings. Besides, a lot of angry Christians recognize that it would be akin to insubordination to be angry with God, so they don't admit it, perhaps even to themselves.

If we don't confess that we are sinners, how can we turn from that sin? And likewise, if we don't express that we are angry (to God, in this case), how can we deal with that anger and submit ourselves again to God's will? In that regard, while Jonah's *attitude* of anger toward God (because God had a different plan for Nineveh than Jonah did) was wrong, Jonah's *confession* of it was necessary. It is the attitude that's wrong, not the confession of it, so if we already have a particular attitude, why not admit it and deal with it?

The other reason that "submission to God's plan" problems so often lead to depression is that there is really no hope in arguing with God about it. He has His plan all worked out, and He hasn't asked for our approval. Bluntly put, *we have to give in to God's plan or fight it and lose.*

Sometimes, Christians give in to God's plan on the outside (because they know the alternative is judgment and unhappiness), but on the inside they really don't believe that God's plan is definitely better than theirs. Knowing they can't win, they hold in their anger, and depression is inevitable.

## I Don't Like This Plan

I once received a call from a young seminary student about to return for his senior year, who told me he'd been depressed for more than a year. He had seen two psychiatrists and was taking antidepressant medication.

The prospect of having one day to cure a depression that had already lasted a full year, resisting medications and psychiatrists, was not what I'd call a very high percentage chance. But he was a friend of a friend, so I agreed to see him.

When he arrived I asked him a question I ask most people who are depressed: "Who are you angry with?"

He said, "Frankly, I feel angry with just about everything: people, trees, birds, wallpaper, you name it."

Well, this was a good start because I have observed that people who are angry with everything are usually angry with the source of everything—God. So we shifted to play-acting therapy that is sometimes helpful in speeding up the therapy process.

I said, "Let's pretend you're talking to God. You be you and I'll be God." (I jumped up and stood on a chair, folded my arms, and waited.) He started to talk and I noticed that he was standing with his arms folded, in exactly the same physical posture as I (God) was.

I interrupted him after a few minutes and said (still playing God), "I see you're standing just like I am. Most people kneel."

He replied rather forcefully, "I don't want to kneel before You!" That was the key and I was able to use it to get him to admit, "I don't like God's plan for me. There are several students who are brighter than me. Some are taller; some are more charismatic speakers. I'm just average and I hate it!"

Identifying the submission problem was about all we had time to do, but the young man didn't like the way he had sounded and went back to seminary to work on not just giving in to God's plan, but embracing it as good and perfect.

## New Areas of Submission

While many of us have gone through times of struggle and submission, I'm not sure that we're ever completely finished with
the battle. I've taught classes about God's goodness and the
need to embrace His plan to live a contented life, and I thought
I'd worked this out in my own life. But I was reminded again
recently that God is *always* working to more fully control our
lives.

One of my daughters had a bad cold and was coughing
almost nonstop. To make matters worse, she has a slight heart
problem that's triggered by many medications, including anti-
histamines and cough medicines, so we couldn't give her
anything for it. So she was up all night coughing, feeling
miserable, and she had two finals at school the next day.

As my wife and I lay in bed praying for her, hour after hour,
and listening to her cough, hour after hour, my wife said, "I'm
getting angry."

"Me too," I admitted.

I realized the next day that my attitude was, "O God, do
what You want to me. I know that will be for the best, but if
You hurt my daughter Your plan needs some improvement."
That was wrong, of course. I had not realized I had been
holding out on God in that area until that incident.

## Resisting a Tidal Wave

Perhaps you're already quite aware of the sovereignty of God,
but just by way of quick review, the word sovereign means
king. God is King; He's the One in control. He can do what He
wants, and indeed, that's the point. God *will* do what He
wishes. Trying to resist God's plan is like trying to resist a
100-foot tidal wave by blowing at it. Blowing would have exactly *zero* effect on the tidal wave's progress, even if you blew hard
and even if you got angry about it.

Some people might also react to a tidal wave by ignoring it, denying that it existed. But they would surely be flattened and swept along if they were in its path, whether or not they had previously acknowledged its power or existence. In the same way, God will do what He will do. And He'll do it with or without our help and agreement. The self-sufficiency of God is another well-established biblical principle. His Word even says that if we don't praise Him, the stones will (Luke 19:40). God does not need us; we need Him.

From this biblical principle we see the appropriate response to God's plan (the tidal wave) is to grab the nearest surfboard and line up in the same direction. When we do, all the power of the wave is behind us and we get quite a ride. But when we become discontent and try to swim against the tidal wave, we are in for a bumpy and unsuccessful trip.

God is our only power source. When we decide to go our own way, we are powerless. It has been wisely said that the successful Christian life can be summarized in one word—obedience.

Of course, your particular plan may not be sinful in essence. It might be, humanly speaking, quite reasonable. But if God's plan is different than yours, then yours is wrong by virtue of the fact that it differs from God's and He is perfect. Your plan, therefore, must be inferior. Don't fight. Switch.

## Why Me, God?

The Bible has many examples of men and women whom God chose and used mightily, but who were subject to times of depression when they became discontented with God's plan. Notice what happened to Elijah. In 1 Kings 19:4 (NIV), Elijah prayed to God that he might die, adding, "I've had enough." Enough of what? The implied answer is: "God, I've had enough of *Your* plan."

Interestingly, Elijah's depression followed the high point of his career. In 1 Kings 18 Elijah contended with the prophets of

Baal, and God miraculously intervened by sending fire from heaven to burn the altar sacrifice. The people of Israel all shouted, "The Lord, He is God," the prophets of Baal were killed, and the long drought was ended. All in one chapter.

It is apparent that Elijah had planned a time of peace, rejoicing, and affirmation after the victory of faith at Mount Carmel. God, on the other hand, planned a time of further testing from evil Queen Jezebel, who sought the prophet's life. In his disagreement with God's plan, Elijah became discontented with living God's kind of life and became depressed, seeking death. Only after God's gentle but persistent prompting under the juniper tree at Horeb was Elijah once more prepared to face life's responsibilities.

Next, notice what happened to Moses in Numbers 11:10-15 (TLB):

> Moses said to the Lord, "Why pick on me, to give me the burden of a people like this? Are they *my* children? Am I their father? Is that why You have given me the job of nursing them along like babies until we get to the land You promised their ancestors? Where am I supposed to get meat for all these people? For they weep to me saying, 'Give us meat!' I can't carry this nation by myself! The load is far too heavy! If You are going to treat me like this, please kill me right now; it will be a kindness! Let me out of this impossible situation!"

Moses was clearly asking, "Why me? Why must I bear the burden of these people?" An important aspect to Moses' depression is that he had assumed a responsibility for the Israelites that was definitely not his, but God's. Taking responsibility for things over which you have no control is a significant cause of discontent depression. It can result not only from making God's responsibility your responsibility, but from taking responsibility for other people's lives and problems as well.

Margaret is a prime example. She was a hard-working Christian woman with a matching reputation. If you wanted anything done, you asked Margaret.

Believe it or not, Margaret's day often began at 3 A.M. She claimed that was the only time she could bake for the eight shut-ins on her list. She also did the linen for the church's communion table at that time of day.

Margaret's invalid mother lived with her and her husband and two teenaged children. Besides all the attention they required, Margaret called her sister—who had had a nervous breakdown—almost daily, telling her what she should do.

Margaret was free with her advice and very well motivated, but she did more than help. She tried to control. She had five children, and the older three had each moved as far away from Mother as possible in order to live their own lives.

When people wouldn't accept Margaret's advice or submit to her control, she became very upset and suffered frequent bouts of depression.

Be aware that when you take responsibility for something or someone, there's always an element of taking control over that person or situation, and only God is really able to do that. You might say only God is "wired" that way, and when people try to do it, they "short out" and often get depressed. Margaret "shorted out" by trying to take responsibility for many lives and problems over which she had no control. When she stopped doing that, her depression stopped as well.

## The Two Josephs

There are, of course, biblical examples of people who willingly submitted to God's plan without attempting to fight it, among them, two Josephs.

The Old Testament Joseph was thrown in a pit, rejected by his brothers, separated from his father and his home, and wrongfully imprisoned. Yet there appears to have been no time of depression. Joseph went where God sent him and apparently did so without complaint.

How could he do that? How could he stay contented? He apparently never wavered in his faith that God was working His plan, and that the best place for Joseph was in the center of it, no matter how far into the pit he was thrown.

If the Old Testament Joseph was cast into a pit deep enough for men to pull him out with long ropes, the New Testament Joseph was in "the pits" so deeply it required an angel to dredge him out. Joseph, the man God chose to be Jesus' earthly father figure, was faced with a difficult situation when he learned that Mary, his espoused wife, was pregnant. In that culture, a betrothal was so formal that it required a divorce to separate the couple, and the death of either rendered the other a widow or widower. Furthermore, unfaithfulness demanded death by public stoning.

Joseph had to decide the fate of his wife. Being a righteous man (Matt. 1:19), he decided it would be best to quietly divorce Mary rather than submit her to judicial procedures. Joseph had a plan of his own, but an angel of the Lord explained to him that God's plan was different. We have no indication of argument or struggle here. Joseph simply abandoned his plan and obeyed God. When he did, God gave him the perfect Son.

Both Josephs contentedly submitted to God's plan and exhibited godly behavior wherever God put them. They found that godly behavior was possible when it began with a godly attitude—submitting to God's plan rather than asserting their own.

# 8

# Love Boat Syndrome

"I didn't mean to, but I accidentally fell in love with my secretary so I guess I have to marry her. I feel bad about having to leave my wife and two kids, but what am I going to do? I didn't mean to do it. I guess these things just happen."

A man who claimed to be a Christian actually said that to me several months ago. Yes, I know. It is weird, but there are a lot of weird things going on out there, especially in regard to the meaning of love.

## Misunderstanding Love

In the culture of the '80s there is rampant misunderstanding about love, usually leading to disappointment, frustration, emotional turmoil, and depression.

We as believers are supposed to be love experts. And yet I've heard some incredibly emotionally illiterate statements recently, many of them from the lips of professing Christians. One question I'm asked fairly often is: "Is it possible to love two women at the same time?" (The answer is, "It depends on what you mean by love.") Another comment I've heard more than once is: "Well, I love her but I don't like her."

I think everyone has asked or at least has heard the question, "How do I know when I'm in love?" The answer most of us have always been given is, "When you're in love, you'll know it." Yet this is not only the wrong answer but a poor one.

## The Love Experts
Christians are supposed to know more about love than unbelievers. If you aren't sure about that, read a few verses from 1 John 4, beginning with verse 7.

> Beloved, let us love one another, for love is from God; and everyone who loves is born of God and knows God. The one who does not love does not know God, for God is love. By this the love of God was manifested in us, that God has sent His only begotten Son into the world that we might live through Him. In this is love, not that we loved God, but that He loved us and sent His Son to be the propitiation for our sins. Beloved, if God so loved us, we also ought to love one another. No one has beheld God at any time; if we love one another, God abides in us, and His love is perfected in us.

Now pay attention to what "we abide in Him and He in us" is paired with in verses 13-17.

> By this we know that we abide in Him and He in us, because He has given us of His Spirit. And we have beheld and bear witness that the Father has sent the Son to be the Saviour of the world. Whoever confesses that Jesus is the Son of God, God abides in him, and he in God. And we have come to know and have believed the love which God has for us. God is love, and the one who abides in love abides in God, and God abides in him. By this, love is perfected with us, that we may have confidence in the day of judgment; because as He is, so also are we in this world.

You may have noticed that the phrase, "God abides in us, and we abide in Him," is paired with a belief in the Father, a belief in the Son, a belief in the Holy Spirit, and with a display of love.

When I first realized that, I was really bowled over. The importance of showing love in the Christian life is, at least in this passage, right up there with believing in the Father, the Son, and the Holy Spirit.

We, as Christians, should be love experts, but what is love? What does it mean? Let's look at a couple of definitions. The first idea someone is going to suggest is that *love is an emotion.* It is affection associated with ecstatic highs, hearing bells or music, losing your appetite, walking in the rain, and two-hour phone calls.

Someone else might say *love is emotional affection,* or caring. You constantly think about the other person; you like being together. You enjoy just looking at him, listening to him, giving to him.

But while love may include emotion and caring, it's not just emotion and caring. And that is already a distinction from what we hear in the "Love Boat" philosophy (which we will get to in a moment).

Another definition we hear for love relates to physical intimacy as in the phrase *making love.* Christians are often called prudes, but it is non-Christians who invented the phrase "making love" as sort of a pseudonym. To them "making love" has become confused with "loving." I've met people who *make* love with three or four different partners a week, but are still incredibly lonely and don't know what love really is. It is obvious that each of these definitions is incomplete.

## What Is Love?

When we first get to know someone, he or she very gradually becomes a friend. That is the best foundation for a loving relationship I know—being friends. Out of the intimacy of friendship, a concern and desire to continue and improve the relationship often develops. It is not a desire to improve your ability to "get," but a desire to improve your ability to "give" and to put the other person's needs above your own. It is a desire to commit yourself to that person and to what is best for that person. The key word here is "commitment"; the others are "giving" and "seeking the highest good."

Ultimately, love is something you decide. It's an act of the will and certainly need not be contrary to common sense. Emotion may not be sensible; emotion may not be permanent; but love is sensible and love is permanent. Sexual attraction may wane and feelings may come and go, but love endures. Of course, love often includes emotion and physical attraction, but primarily *it is a commitment to the highest good for the loved one.*

## The Love Boat

The strength of this definition can be shown when we compare and contrast it to the Love Boat definition of love that is so intensely permeating our society. In case you've just come back from 10 years on the moon, I'm referring to the popular weekly television program called "The Love Boat."

On "The Love Boat" you see the same formula over and over again, so much that you begin to think and expect that what happens on that cruise ship is normal. Here's "The Love Boat" scenario: First, two people meet and they fall in love. Instantly! Second, there's action (they go to bed that night or the next night at the latest). Third, they back into a decision. On the way off the boat, they tell the captain, "We're getting married!" Friends, *emotion* followed by *action* followed by *decision* is the Love Boat Syndrome and it's exactly backward to what God's Word teaches. It is also exactly backward to anything that promotes stable relationships and psychological health. Because we're basing so many of our emotions on this backward approach to life, our relationships aren't lasting and our divorce rate is exploding.

Do you remember the old Sunday School song we used to sing about building one's house upon the rock? Why didn't the wise man build his house upon the sand? Because with no secure foundation it would surely fall flat in times of storm, as the foolish man's indeed did. Relationships built on emotion are just like that house with no foundation. Emotions are temporary.

Your emotions, mine, and everyone else's are reflexes. When I hit just the right spot on my knee, my leg is going to jerk. That's a physical or external reflex. We've all got them. An emotion is an internal reflex, an internal response to people and circumstances.

The people in your life—are they the same this year as they were last year? Are they the same this month as they were last month? Are they the same today as they were yesterday? How about your circumstances? Are they the same this year as they were last year?

If emotions are reflexes to people and circumstances, are they going to remain the same? There isn't any way that they can, because the people and circumstances around us are changing more rapidly than they ever have, probably in all of history. Perhaps you've heard statistics on the rate of change during our lifetime. Of all the technology that the world now knows, 80 percent of it has been invented or discovered in the last 10 years. In terms of transportation, law, and education, we live in a time of incredibly rapid flux. Surely the pressure and rapid change affect our emotions and cause them to change frequently.

Because of our rapidly changing emotions, let's look more closely at what happens when a relationship is built on the sand of the Love Boat Syndrome (basing a decision on emotion). First, you have an emotion, a strong affection for someone. She's on your mind constantly and when you're with her you're

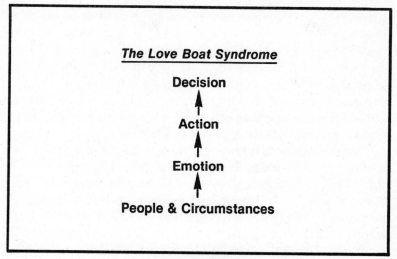

FIGURE 8-1

happy. When you're apart you feel sick. If, because of that emotion, you go to bed and get married, what happens when this emotion is gone? The house crumbles. The decision no longer has any foundation.

A decision seems to make perfect sense when it is built on the sand of emotion, but it makes no sense when the sand moves, and the sand of emotion always moves. When it does, your spouse may come to you and say, "But Sweetheart, I just don't love you anymore." And that is precisely how many Love Boat relationships die, even among professing Christians.

That brings me to the problem of believers in Jesus Christ marrying unbelievers. Talk about depression! What a horrible condition in which to live.

I'm almost embarrassed to state something so obvious, but because so many people overlook it, I reemphasize that a believer in Jesus Christ is not to participate in a loving relationship with someone who is not a believer. The Bible is quite clear when it says, "Be ye not unequally yoked together with unbelievers: for what fellowship hath righteousness with unrighteousness? And what communion hath light with darkness?" (2 Cor. 6:14, KJV) If love develops out of close friendship, then that close friendship must be with someone of the same belief. (Of course, if a believer is already married to an unbeliever, it is God's will that they stay married as long as the unbelieving partner chooses not to separate—1 Cor. 7:12-16.)

There are more differences between believers and unbelievers than where they spend Sunday mornings. Their entire view of the universe is fundamentally different. The believer puts Christ at the center, and obeying and magnifying Him becomes his purpose for living. On the other hand, the unbeliever is at the center of his own universe, and his purpose for living can vary from one day to the next. Being trapped in such a stress-filled situation is depressing thousands and thousands of believers every year.

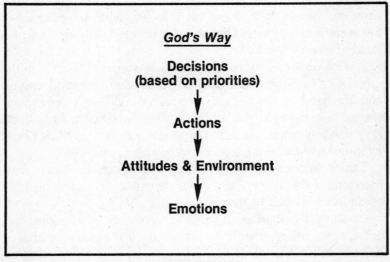

FIGURE 8-2

## God's Way of Loving

Loving relationships don't have to be unstable. While the first diagram (figure 8-1, p. 77) showed love and relationship decisions based on the most changing aspects of life, the second (figure 8-2, p. 78) shows that God's way is really the reverse of the Love Boat.

God's love most definitely is *based on choice*. Deuteronomy 7:7-8 says, "The Lord did not set His love on you nor *choose* you because you were more in number than any of the peoples, for you were fewest of all peoples, but [simply] *because* the Lord loved you" (italics added). And Deuteronomy 10:15 adds: "Yet on your fathers did the Lord set His affection to love them, and He *chose* their descendants after them, even you above all peoples" (italics added). God's love is based on choice. He decided to love you. He chose to do so.

Second, God's love is *constant*. Psalm 42:8 (KJV) says, "The Lord will command His loving-kindness in the daytime and in the night His song shall be with me." And Psalm 89:33 (KJV) says, "My loving-kindness will I not utterly take from him, nor suffer My faithfulness to fail." In other words, God's love always stays the same. (By the way, there are many verses for each of these points, but I'm just giving you a couple.)

Third, God's love involves *action*. Jeremiah 31:3 reads, "I have loved you with an everlasting love. Therefore I have *drawn* you with loving-kindness" (italics added). John 3:16 (KJV) says, "For God so loved the world that He *gave* His only begotten Son" (italics added). First He loved, then He showed it by His actions.

## Acceptance

God's love also includes *acceptance*. This means not trying to change the person before you love him. Romans 5:8 says, "God demonstrates His own love toward us, in that while we were yet sinners, Christ died for us." He loved us when we were sinners, when we were incomplete. Not because we earned it and not because we were forgiven. He didn't love us because He forgave us; He forgave us because He already loved us. Ephesians 2:4-5 adds, "God, being rich in mercy, because of His great love with which He loved us, even when we were dead in our transgressions, made us alive together with Christ." He loved us even when we were dead in sin. He accepts us where we are. This is an absolute necessity of real love, and its absence causes a lot of broken relationships.

Failure to accept your loved one's personality can be an ongoing cause of depression, producing repeated cycles of emotional stress year after year.

Marianne was an achiever. She was always taking one course or another to improve herself or to just broaden her horizons. Because of her excellence in teaching she'd been promoted to resource adviser for the entire school district. To Marianne, there was no such thing as settling for something "good enough to get by." She kept house perfectly; she played the piano perfectly; she selected her wardrobe perfectly. She was a genuine believer in being the best she could be.

Marianne's husband was a different story altogether. He gave new meaning to the phrase "laid-back and easygoing." She tried every technique known to mankind to get her husband to better himself, to advance, or to even wear one of the new shirts she bought him. But Ralph was happy being exactly who he was. He didn't have a care in the world. (She worried, why should he?) And he didn't budge an inch from where he was. I mean that both figuratively (he never changed), and literally (as in, he never moved from the couch).

Marianne was definitely not content to accept her husband as he was, and the more her attempts to change him were frustrated, the more she got depressed. She needed to learn to accept her husband, rather than try to change him. And acceptance involves conscious decision.

## Deciding to Love

The whole issue of deciding to love and accepting the loved one "as is" sounds like a new idea to many of us, but it's not new to most of the world. In Eastern countries, including the Middle East and India, many marriages are still being arranged by parents without the couple's input, let alone romance. A young person who suddenly finds him or herself married to a perfect stranger, (or even to a less-than-perfect stranger), has a very important decision to make. If that marriage has any hope of happiness, each must decide to *accept* the spouse the way he or she is, and *then* decide to love.

In Western countries, where marriage is based heavily on emotion and romance, this decision to love is still necessary. It is often made only when the temporary "in love" feeling fades, which used to occur around the sixth or seventh year of marriage. But now the feeling seems to be fading much sooner if the growing divorce rate is any clue.

At some point in a lasting relationship there must be a decision to love. As we have said, emotions are just reflexes. Many depressed people are depressed because they feel emotional affection ("in love") toward one person but have commitment (and often a marriage and children) toward another. They feel trapped. They followed their emotions into a maze and now the only way out is to make a decision based on priorities rather than a decision based on emotions.

The opening illustration in this chapter was of a man who was experiencing a very pleasant emotion, called "love." It is unfortunate to feel that feeling for someone when you are married to someone else, as was the case in his situation. But the situation goes from unfortunate to catastrophic (and depressing) when you make decisions based on that or any other temporary emotion.

I frequently hear people say, "I don't know if I really love my husband (or wife) anymore. I'm just not sure if it's real." Persons who don't know for sure are looking for some emotion to validate their reality. They are saying to themselves, "Things are real only when I feel an emotion about them." But when we understand that emotions are only reflexes and always changing, then we can see that judging something solely by what emotion it elicits is foolish and leads to unstable decisions and depression. The appropriate question, then, is not, "Do I really love my husband?" but rather, "Have I decided to love him?"

# 9

# Guilt, Grace, and God's Gift

As we conclude this section on specific conflicts that can often lead to depression, we come now to the conflict between guilt and grace. Guilt, of course, means "You've done something bad," and grace is God's response to your guilt. Grace says, "I love you anyway and give you something good that you don't deserve."

Guilt has two aspects, either of which can exist without the other. The two aspects are "being guilty" (also known as judicial guilt), and "feeling guilty" (also called shame). If you exceed the speed limit you *are* guilty of breaking that law, but you may not *feel* guilty.

I think of one of my patients who had a terrible problem with guilt feelings. At one point she came into my office after feeling overwhelming guilt for three days—about spilling shampoo. It was her shampoo and she spilled it in her own tub, but she felt guilty nonetheless! She was not judicially guilty of breaking any law or commandment, but the emotional guilt was there just the same.

When a person acknowledges his sin and asks Jesus to be his

Saviour and pay the penalty for that sin, (thereby removing his guilt), Jesus does exactly that. The Bible teaches that we are declared "not guilty," that we stand completely righteous in God's sight when we place our trust in Christ. Romans 8:1 says, "There is therefore now no condemnation for those who are in Christ Jesus."

As wonderful as that is, it only removes our condition of guilt, not our guilt feelings. Many believers say, "I know God has forgiven me, but I still feel terrible about it," or, "I know God forgave me but I can't forgive myself."

As you may imagine, it is very hard for guilt and grace to live together in the same spirit. Tremendous conflict develops, and often depression is a consequence.

## Bondage of Guilt

Sally is a recent Christian who still suffers from nagging guilt. On a spiritual level we could say that Satan was unable to keep Sally from accepting God's gracious gift of forgiveness and adoption. But when Satan could no longer keep Sally in the condition of "being" guilty, he settled for having her "feel" guilty. Feeling guilty kept Sally from the free, easy, and open communication and relationship with the Father that she could have enjoyed. And when Sally withdrew from the Father because she felt guilty, she cut herself off from her only power source. Consequently, she experienced little victory and joy in her Christian life.

When Satan can get someone to live a guilt-focused life rather than a grace-focused life, that person's testimony and effectiveness as a soldier of the Cross is at least partially nullified. Rather than being a spiritual block to psychological success, this guilt-grace problem is usually a psychological block to spiritual success. Though we are truly right before God (having been forgiven and declared righteous), we don't feel it and, therefore, may not act it.

## Perfect before God

I know that some people will question whether we are really "right" before God if we withdraw from Him and do not experience complete joy and victory. In answer to that, it is important that we understand that our acceptance before God is total and absolute, based on Christ's total and absolutely perfect sacrifice. God already sees His children as perfect. That condition cannot be improved on. If our behavior were suddenly perfected between now and noon tomorrow, God wouldn't love us any more, after a whole year of perfect behavior, than He does right now.

Yes, our behavior needs to improve, but not to gain any more of God's acceptance. And our behavior can improve, but only out of a motivation of love and gratitude and a desire to be more Christlike—not out of fear. Romans 8:15 says, "For you have not received a spirit of slavery leading to fear again, but you have received a spirit of adoption as sons by which we cry out, 'Abba! Father!' "

To correct the problem of feeling guilty when we are really forgiven, we must recognize that God's forgiveness is total and perfect. Christ paid the penalty once for all time according to verses like Hebrews 9:28 that tell us He was "offered *once* to bear the sins of many" (italics added). He has already paid for the sins you'll commit today, next week, and for the rest of your lifetime. Right now you've got a credit balance equal to what your total debt will be.

Don't let Satan convince you that God is still angry with you for your sin. God sees only Christ's blood, not your sin. That's what redemption is all about. It is true that you need to come to God in repentance to restore your part of the relationship—to turn back to God, but *He never turned away from you!* If you are a child of God, then Romans 8:1 applies to you. "There is therefore now *no condemnation* for those who are in Christ Jesus" (italics added).

You may be accustomed to asking for daily forgiveness by quoting the familiar 1 John 1:9 (KJV), which reads, "If we confess our sins, He is faithful and just to forgive us our sins, and to cleanse us from all unrighteousness." This is a good evangelistic verse, but in my opinion it says nothing about daily "please forgive me's."

What does "confess" mean? If you were sitting in a courtroom and the district attorney said, "Confess!" what does he want you to say? "I'm sorry. Please forgive me"? No, he wants you to say, "I'm guilty. I did a wrong thing." Many people, including myself, believe that acknowledgment of our sinful state (i.e., confession) is what we do when we ask for salvation. (As in, "God, I am a sinner.") As for acknowledgment of our sins and repentance after each individual sin, it seems that, "God, I've sinned again. I'm sorry. Thank You that You forgave me for that one too," is a more theologically accurate prayer in terms of our guilt and God's grace. It is also a far more positive experience to thank God for His forgiveness and talk about His goodness than to dwell on our badness.

## Guilt as a Motivator

I've known many well-meaning pastors who don't seem to know how to end their messages without trying to make the congregation feel guilty. Christ died to remove our guilt, so why are we trying to dump it back on people again?

The answer these pastors often give is that they are trying to motivate behavior change. But guilt feelings are poor motivators. They make you feel bad, but they don't change your behavior.

I'll prove it to you. How many times have you felt guilty about not spending enough time reading the Bible? Probably many times because guilt motivation is not strong enough to permanently change your behavior. People change their Bible reading habits most often when they realize they are happier and their lives more powerful as they read the Scriptures or because they love the Lord so much they can't get enough of His Word.

Parents often try to motivate and control their children with the use of guilt and, unfortunately, it often works. I say unfortunately, because, though it is effective, it is also terribly destructive. Virtually every depressed patient who is suffering from false guilt (guilt "feelings" without actually "being" guilty) has been significantly influenced to feel this way by parents using guilt as a means of child control. These parents have controlled their children at the expense of making them neurotic, depressed, and possessors of a crippling self-image, a self-image that says, "I can't do anything right."

I've referred to what we can do spiritually to help the guilt problem, but many depressed people already acknowledge the theological accuracy of forgiveness. Their problem is more related to psychological guilt, greatly affecting self-worth.

## The Parent inside You

The self-valuing system that gives us our feelings of positive or negative worth comes from the way significant adults relate to us when we are children.

When we were growing up we had parents and other significant adults (grandparents, aunts, uncles, teachers) tell us, "This is good," "This is bad," "You are good," "You are bad," "Naughty girl," "Good boy." These reinforcements, both positive and negative, unconsciously add up in our minds to determine what kind of a person we think we are.

While a part of the human conscience is clearly God-given, it is largely shaped by our parents. We carry this internalized parent around in our heads all the time, evaluating every moral step we make. The problem is that the internalized parent is not perfect. In some cases it is overly rigid and condemning.

One depressed pastor told me, "I was not affirmed for much

of anything in my youth. No one encouraged me, and I generally had the feeling there wasn't much good about me. I was desperately afraid I might do something wrong, so I did very little that wasn't required and I really sweat over everything I did.

"Even the day I graduated from college with the highest grades of any man in that school, I went up for my award with my head down and my shoulders hunched. I was afraid to appear proud. It was agony for me to have to go up there."

This man had very rigid parents. Not mean, but never positive or affirming. They pointed out everything he did wrong, but figured he shouldn't be praised for doing what was right—so they didn't. He never knew there was anything "right" about him.

Barbara, another example, had a Ph.D. in chemistry and was one of the most beautiful women that you or I would ever be likely to meet. But her self-image was negative because she had a sister who was even more beautiful. If a man would ask her for a date she would get very angry and say, "Who put you up to this? I know you don't want to go out with me! Did my father pay you to ask me out?" And the man would walk away saying, "She's pretty but she's really flaky."

Unfortunately, Barbara evaluated herself, not objectively, but subjectively—constantly comparing herself with her sister. She saw herself as "the ugly one," not because anyone ever told her that, but because she never received the attention her sister did.

We all have a self-evaluating part of us. Imagine for a moment that when you went into the bookstore to buy this book you saw your child's Sunday School teacher selecting material for her class. What would happen if she came up to you and said, "Oh, what a delight to see you here! You've made my day! Just seeing you somehow seems to make the sun shine a little brighter and it makes me want to whistle a tune! You're one of my favorite people in the whole world! God has really blessed us to have you live in this town with us! Of all the people in the world . . ." and on she goes. I'm sure you would begin to wonder, "What's wrong with this lady?" and start inching your way toward the door. People who say things like that tend to make us very uncomfortable.

This virtually universal uneasiness with such blatantly positive statements about ourselves illustrates one of the most fascinating mysteries of psychology. Everyone longs to mean so much to someone that we could make their day brighter. Wouldn't it be wonderful if someone loved us enough to want to whistle a tune whenever they saw us? It sounds nice, but if we *really* want that, why does it make us so uneasy?

The answer is that we reject overly positive statements because we don't believe them. Each of us has a self-image, an estimation of who we are or would like to be, and of how much we are worth. If we hear things that contradict that estimation of ourselves, we reject them, no matter how much we would like them to be true.

Whether our self-valuing system is accurate or not, (and it almost never is), it nonetheless affects our emotional lives, relationships with God and other people, occupations, attitudes, and ambitions. But what does God have to say about our self-worth?

## What Is Man?
As evangelical adults, it is important to study self-worth from God's perspective rather than our own, and that requires checking out the Scriptures on the matter. In Matthew 10:31 we are reminded that God's people are of more value than many sparrows, and in Ephesians 1:4 we are told, "He [God] chose us in Him before the foundation of the world." Of course, the Christian's greatest worth to God is shown in His act of love at Calvary (John 3:16).

Genesis 1:24-31 is not quoted as often in regard to man's worth, but the passage contains some important truths.

> Then God said, "Let the earth bring forth living creatures after their kind, cattle and creeping things and beasts of the earth after their kind"; and it was so. And God made the beasts of the earth after their kind, and cattle after their kind, and everything that creeps on the ground after its kind; and God saw that it was good (vv. 24-25).

## Man the Ruler

How did God make the animals? To multiply after their kind. This is important because in verses 26-31 God says,

> "Let Us make man in Our image, according to Our likeness; and let them rule over the fish of the sea and over the birds of the sky and over the cattle and over all the earth, and over every creeping thing that creeps on the earth." And God created man in His own image, in the image of God He created him; male and female He created them. And God blessed them; and God said to them, "Be fruitful and multiply, and fill the earth, and subdue it; and rule over the fish of the sea and over the birds of the sky, and everything that moves on the earth." Then God said, "Behold, I have given you every plant yielding seed that is on the surface of all the earth, and every tree which has fruit yielding seed; it shall be food to you; and to every beast of the earth and to every bird of the sky, and to every thing that moves on the earth which has life, I have given every green plant for food"; and it was so. And God saw all that He had made, and behold, it was very good.

Though all Creation was deemed "very good" by God, a clear difference is noted between animals, who were made after their own kind, and man, who was made not after his own kind, but in the image of God. *Each of us is made in God's image.*

We also discover that *man was created by God to rule.* Though man's absolute dominion over the earth was lost at the Fall, his authority will be returned during the Millennium when God's children will assist Him in His kingdom rule (2 Tim. 2:12). The very same you and I who consider ourselves of little value will actually help God rule. We are called Christ's ambassadors (2 Cor. 5:20)—what a tremendous statement of our worth!

According to Psalm 8, we are made just a little lower than the Elohim. Elohim can be translated God, gods, or angels, and it's really anybody's guess as to what was really intended. The point is that man is of great worth, whether it is a little lower than God or a little lower than the angels.

In Ephesians 2:10 we are told, "We are His [God's] workmanship." Bill Gothard suggests that "workmanship" be translated "masterpiece." What is an artist's masterpiece? It's his very best, the one creation he's happiest with and proudest of. That is the word used in Ephesians 2:10. We are His masterpiece, created in Christ Jesus.

We are so valuable to God that He numbers the hairs of our heads (Matt. 10:30). We must be very important for Him to bother doing that, because He has to come up with a new count every day, coming or going. Just think of the man-hours required for a job like that. We must surely be valuable to God.

## Man the Worm

We have looked at the good news, the positive verses that say we are worthy. But there is another message to look at, one that frankly isn't as much fun to read about.

The negative message about our worth is a real part of Christianity, and whether we feel like it or not, we can't take a biblical view of self-esteem and look only at the verses that please us. First, let's look at the Old Testament:

"If even the moon has no brightness and the stars are not pure in His sight, how much less man, that maggot, and the son of man, that worm!" (Job 25:5-6)

"Behold, I am vile; what shall I answer Thee?" (Job 40:4, KJV)

"When I consider Thy heavens . . . what is man, that Thou dost take thought of him? And the son of man, that Thou dost care for him?" (Ps. 8:3-4)

"But I am a worm, and not a man, a reproach of men, and despised by the people" (Ps. 22:6).

"Look to the rock from which you were hewn, and to the hole of the pit from which you were dug" (Isa. 51:5, NKJV).

"The heart is deceitful above all things, and desperately wicked; who can know it?" (Jer. 17:9, KJV)

In the New Testament we find the following:

"I know that in me (that is, in my flesh,) dwelleth no good thing" (Rom. 7:18, KJV).

"Not that we are adequate in ourselves to consider anything as coming from ourselves" (2 Cor. 3:5).

"It is a trustworthy statement, deserving full acceptance, that Christ Jesus came into the world to save sinners; among whom I am foremost of all" (1 Tim. 1:15).

A conflict is apparent between the "Man the Ruler" verses and the "Man the Worm" verses. The tension we feel between the "warm" feelings and the "worm" feelings is really a result of the basic need for acceptance and a sense of worth, a need which is good, natural, and right. However, the real conflict arises because the human and culturally acceptable ways of feeling worthy—bragging, boasting, putting others down—and God's way of making us worthy are greatly opposed. God doesn't want us to lift up ourselves. Instead He wants us to acknowledge our emptiness so He can fill and use us.

Many verses say that we are not to lift up ourselves, including Luke 14:11, "For everyone who exalts himself shall be humbled," and James 4:6, "God is opposed to the proud." Christian parents who are always putting down their children, giving them inappropriate guilt feelings, may unfortunately think they are doing right because of these verses. And what damage they can do!

A balanced self-image is necessary. We are not totally worthless, but neither are we totally useful and worthy without God's molding and filling. The Lord works in us to make us usable, and if we insist that we are useless, then we are actually going against His plan.

Without God we can do nothing. But with Him we can do anything. It is not right or righteous to view yourself or any other human being—God's masterpiece of creation—as junk or defective merchandise. For when God fills us, He gives us the gift of adequacy and worth and removes the burden of uselessness and guilt that often leads to depression.

# Part 3

# Curing Depression

# 10

---

# Things You Can Do to Help Yourself

As we have said several times, the vast majority of all depressions are the result of unidentified or unlabeled emotions. The cure for the depression, then, is to find and label the emotion you didn't consciously notice the first time it occurred and outwardly express it.

## Find the Right Tool

Whether your depression is severe, lasting many months, or mild, you've still got one or more emotions stuck in your emotional pipeline, and you need a handle or a tool to pull it out and, in doing so, unplug the system. That handle or tool is the *specific* name of the emotion. The more specific the name, the better grip you can get on the emotion that's stuck, and the more likely you are to dislodge it.

Notice how many levels, from general to specific expression, occur in the following dialogue between depressed person and counselor.

COUNSELOR: Well, Betty, what seems to be the problem?

BETTY: Oh, everything!

COUNSELOR: Everything?

BETTY: I just don't see any reason to live anymore.

COUNSELOR: You sound pretty upset.

BETTY: I *am* upset!

COUNSELOR: What about?

BETTY: I don't know.

COUNSELOR: Any idea when it started?

BETTY: I was all right last week.

COUNSELOR: Uh-huh.

BETTY: I remember I went to a party Friday night and I was OK then. I was looking forward to going and everything.

COUNSELOR: And how about Saturday?

BETTY: I didn't feel much of anything Saturday—the blahs, you know.

COUNSELOR: I wonder if something upset you at the party?

BETTY: I don't remember anything—oh, wait—I was upset at one of my girlfriends Friday night. I had forgotten that.

COUNSELOR: Did she do something to make you angry?

BETTY: Yes, she sure did. She knows I like this guy, Dan, and she played Ping-Pong with him for an hour while I sat off in the corner by myself. I guess that sounds kind of childish, doesn't it? I knew she wasn't trying to steal Dan or anything, and she's a real good friend.

COUNSELOR: So because you thought the feeling was somehow not very mature, you didn't tell her about it.

BETTY: Yeah, but I had forgotten I was angry until now. Could that little thing have made me depressed this week?

Yes, it could have. You'll notice as we peel back the emotional layers in this dialogue, Betty at first was only aware of feeling depressed—but that was just the outer surface. Underneath that was the blahs or a shutting off of all feeling. Beneath that was "upset," a rather elementary word in the area of emotions because it is so vague it could apply to almost anything.

When she started to get specific, Betty noticed she was angry.

And when she looked more closely at that anger she saw she was angry with a particular friend for one particular activity. It's also likely that if we would peel away another emotional layer, we would see that underneath the anger was possibly a feeling of inferiority that she was not able to loosen up at the party and mix with people. Or maybe a feeling of rejection that the young man, Dan, had picked her girlfriend to play Ping-Pong with. Or the original feeling could have been disappointment that the evening hadn't gone the way she'd hoped.

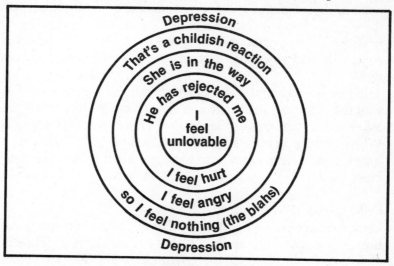

**FIGURE 10-1**

As we see in figure 10-1, depression is on the outside and immediately visible. Only as we begin to peel away the emotional layers can we see the many emotions existing underneath the depression and covered up by it.

The best cure for depression is to figure out what was the last emotion you didn't deal with and deal with it. Often just labeling the emotion is enough to produce immediate relief. When it isn't, then it may require either an outward expression of the emotion or digging deeper to find what emotion lies beneath it (such as Betty's feeling of rejection lying beneath her feeling of anger).

## Detective Dialogue

Is it really as easy to find the cause of the emotional logjam as the previous dialogue seems to indicate? The honest answer is sometimes yes, sometimes no. The more recent the depression (the past few days or weeks), the likelier you can find the hidden emotion by conducting a detective dialogue with yourself. By the way, if that sounds like a game, it *is* fun and rewarding to find the hidden emotion and, frankly, it's one of the most rewarding and enjoyable aspects of a psychologist's work as well.

If you are feeling down this afternoon and you weren't that way this morning, or even if you've been down for a few days, ask yourself, "When was the last time I remember feeling good? When was the first time I remember feeling bad?" Then piece together the events in between to determine the source of your blues.

## Self-analysis

Look for conflicts or negative emotions. Very often one situation will come to your mind almost immediately. Though almost everyone responds to the first idea with, "No, it couldn't have been that," it *could* have, and probably was. It *is* usually the first thing that comes to mind.

Of course, the longer someone has been depressed, the more deeply buried the emotion and the harder it is to do self-analysis. Therefore, the longer someone has been depressed, the likelier it is that they will need outside help to uncover the hidden emotion(s).

Let's look at a couple more examples to demonstrate more clearly what it's like to unravel short-term depressions.

Carl is a gentle man in a middle-management position. He's a responsible guy who tries to be friendly and get along with everyone. The other day he said to me:

CARL: I don't know quite how it happened, but I'm feeling down again.

DR. T: Were you OK last week?

CARL: Yes, I felt really good last week.

DR. T: Tell me about your week.

CARL: It was OK. Sunday I went out to dinner with my in-laws. They took me out for my birthday.

DR. T: Uh-huh, what happened?

CARL: They were their usual selves. My father-in-law is so negative. I hate to say it, but how a man can be so opinionated and critical while being so ignorant, I'll never know!

DR. T: You sound kind of angry.

CARL: I guess I am. He treats me like no one else in the world treats me. I really can't stand it.

DR. T: And this was supposed to be your birthday party.

CARL: Yeah—happy birthday! Honestly. He's the only guy I know who I'd sometimes really like to punch out.

DR. T: But what did you really do?

CARL: Nothing. It was supposed to be a celebration and I didn't want to make trouble.

DR. T: So you held in your anger.

CARL: Can you believe it! I did it again. I held it in and got depressed. When will I ever learn?

DR. T: Sounds like you made trouble after all.

CARL: Yeah, for myself. You keep telling me to express my anger in a loving and direct way whenever possible, but I blew it that time.

DR. T: Still feeling down?

CARL: No, but I've got to start noticing these emotions when they happen.

Carl could have unraveled his own depression by playing back his mental tapes of the last several days and looking for the cause of the blockage. Plus, of course, he could have prevented the depression altogether by noticing his anger when it happened, instead of burying it.

Linda was a young mother with some very significant physical limitations. It took the greater part of her mental energy just to cope with the physical pain she endured so often. She also suffered from periods of sudden depression that she couldn't figure out and which we worked on together for quite some time. This was not a 30-minute cure, but the following conversation was rather significant in finally preventing the recurring depressions.

DR. T: You know, it seems to me like another depression has immediately followed a very hectic time when both children were demanding attention, plus your physical pain, plus other pressures such as the phone or expecting company.

LINDA: Yes, I just hate that.

DR. T: Anger?

LINDA: Way past anger, it's rage. And depression seems to immediately follow it. I guess I've been shoving that anger inside to control it, rather than explode.

DR. T: Yes, I think so too. With what do you suppose you're angry?

LINDA: I don't know but I hate that situation.

DR. T: Maybe you hate being limited.

LINDA: Boy, yes. That's definitely it.

DR. T: And maybe angry at God who made you limited.

LINDA: Yes.

Once Linda knew what emotions were taking place she was able to work on expressing them (to God in this particular case), and to begin working on some of the underlying attitudes that caused the emotions to exist in the first place.

## Finding Godly Ways to Release Emotions

If noticing emotions is essential to breaking out of depression or preventing its return, releasing or expressing those emotions is just as essential, and for the Christian, releasing negative emotions in a Christlike way is an important goal.

Ephesians 4:15 is God's guideline for communication. We are to "speak the truth in love." Like all of God's principles, this one really works. You can say anything when you pair it with the message, "I love you" or "I respect you," or at least, "I'd like to be able to love you."

Remember that you are responsible to say what you have to say in as loving and godly a way possible. But you are *not* responsible for how people react to you. That is between them and God. Unfortunately, many people avoid saying things they need to say because they can't control the other person's reaction. How they react is *their choice*, however. Not yours.

One way to help your conversation appear less like an attack is to use the words "I feel" rather than "you did" or "you made me feel." The word "you" sounds like an attack and usually triggers the listener's automatic antiballistic missile system.

A good introductory paragraph might be, "I've been feeling some things that I've not been sharing with you and that could hurt our relationship, so I felt like I should talk with you about them. They are *my* feelings and *my* responsibility. I'm not blaming *you*. I'm just confessing."

## Destructive Relationships and Situations

Another significant step people can take to end their depressions is to back out of or change destructive relationships and situations.

I remember being caught up in a destructive relationship with a girl while in college. My brother once wisely commented to me, "It seems you can't live with her and you can't live without her." That's how I felt. We had strong feelings for each other, but in many ways I was just not what she wanted and she was not what I wanted. So we fought constantly trying to change each other. I'm thankful that after only a couple of months I saw the light and found the courage to "end the relationship forever and ever, world without end, in perpetuity." I was free.

I'm not advocating leaving your husband or wife, but many situations and people will never change, and the only way out is to realize it and get away. I strongly advise that if a relationship (other than marriage) is making you permanently miserable, consider living without it.

The standard response is, "I don't want to make trouble." But people don't realize they've already got trouble and it's going to get worse, not better, if action isn't taken.

Family business and multiple or extended family living arrangements are prime examples. A live-in relative is a frequent cause of stress. The only way such a living arrangement can ever work is if: (1) rules are laid out very clearly at the beginning, (2) no one accepts the responsibility for anyone else's life, (3) communication is wide open, and (4) the people are unusually mature.

When families are involved in the same business, people often put the appearance of peace, or future financial prosperity above emotional health. This is a mistake.

I talked with a woman whose husband worked with his dad in a plumbing business. She answered the phones and handled most of the paperwork, but mother-in-law retained part of the bookkeeping duties.

Well, mother-in-law never did like daughter-in-law and treated her like you wouldn't treat your pet pig. Unfortunately, the son had always been a passive fellow, so whenever mother-in-law demanded a multiple family gathering, or father-in-law demanded son to work, the daughter-in-law lost any control over her own family life. Consequently, she became very depressed.

Fortunately, her husband loved her enough to finally take a stand with his family. He set up rules and said if they weren't kept, they would leave the business and the town. "My wife," he said, "is most important here, and I don't need this business or this aggravation to survive."

That was one situation where change took place without having to leave, but the *willingness* to leave, if necessary (or throw someone out, or fire someone), seems to be an essential ingredient.

I know it's often said that you can't run away from your problems, but I'm not sure I agree. Many problems *are* localized and leaving can be a smart survival technique. I know that if a tiger walked in my office door, I'd leave and feel good about my escape.

## Be Nice to Yourself

In chapter 5 on childhood maps of the world we referred to the sentences we say to ourselves. Many of these sentences are adopted from things our parents said to us or attitudes our parents had about us when we were young.

A part of each of us is still a frightened child, needing love and comfort. When we get depressed, we are more likely to hear from that frightened child within us and more likely to feel those childhood feelings.

When fears come to the surface, you *can* help yourself by noticing how you respond. Do you get angry with yourself? Do you call yourself names? Do you say things to yourself like, "You can never do anything right!" or "You're hopeless"? If you do, then you are making matters worse.

A frightened child needs comfort, not criticism. If you saw a father kicking his little boy because he was afraid to try something, you wouldn't think much of Dad, would you? Why would the model be any different for you when a part of you is frightened? Don't criticize. Comfort and encourage. Many more fears are overcome through encouragement and edification than are conquered through threats and put-downs. Don't put yourself down. Talk to yourself exactly as you would expect to hear a loving, patient parent talk to a frightened child.

## Budget Your Troops

Earlier in the book I referred to units of emotional and physical energy as "troops." You can help prevent depressions or help your recovery by keeping an eye on how you spend your troops.

If you are depressed, you have a significantly depleted troop supply and this means, for one thing, you can't do everything you'd like. Your recovery will come much faster if you'll learn to say no.

Troops, or emotional and physical energy, must be deployed or budgeted in the same way you budget household expenses. If you have 50 troops worth of available energy and 75 troops worth of things to do today, you're either going to have to say no to 25 troops worth of activities or borrow from tomorrow's troops. Beware of borrowing from tomorrow's troops. It catches up with you after a while, just like the misuse of credit.

One of the first things to do when you are significantly depressed is to reduce your required expenditure of troops (stresses, responsibilities, things to do), to a point where you have enough energy to cope at that lower level of activity.

Cutting back is not easy. Dozens of well-meaning friends will tell you that you've got to keep busy. They don't realize you've got a heavy troop debt to repay from recent weeks, months, or years of spending more emotional energy than you really had.

## Use Spiritual Resources

I want to be careful here not to imply a message of condemnation, but I *do* want to include this exhortation: Be as close to God as you can. Avail yourself of all spiritual resources. Read the Bible daily. Acknowledge your needs. Pray. Praise God and focus on His goodness, faithfulness, and love.

You say you are doing all that and are still depressed? That's fine—your depression is an emotional blockage and not a spiritual problem. But some people get depressed whenever they aren't depending on God's Spirit to fill and energize them. It would, therefore, be foolish not to at least ask, "How is my devotional life? Am I in good relationship and close fellowship with the Father?"

If you become aware of spiritual need, put energy and time into improving your spiritual condition. It could significantly help your depression and it certainly couldn't hurt.

# 11

# Depression and Psychological Counseling

Most people are susceptible to occasional "down" times. As long as these are fairly brief and not too intense, there is no reason to seek professional counseling. What's more, if you can go back and figure out what emotion you've repressed, and by feeling and expressing it relieve the emotional logjam, then you have been your own "outside help."

## Who Needs Professional Help?

The obvious *general* answer to this question is that you need help if you can't handle the emotional problem by yourself. But not being able to handle something yourself is hard to admit. In fact, the Bible indicates that man's desire for self-sufficiency is his most basic sin. You will remember that Satan used that very ploy when he tempted Adam and Eve in the Garden of Eden. And we've been tempted with it ever since.

The *specific* answer to the question of needing professional help is a very personal and individual decision, but here are some guidelines that might be helpful:

*First*, it's important to remember that a week-old depression is

100 times faster and easier (and cheaper!) to cure than a year-old depression. Thus, if you have been depressed for more than a month, talk to someone about it.

*Second*, serious depression often affects your ability to function. If you start to miss work or perform poorly because of preoccupation, or when you feel increasingly unsure of your ability to do things you could normally do without difficulty, your life is being affected and you should seek help.

*Third*, if thoughts of suicide settle in your mind and you seriously begin to think about how you might kill yourself, it is time to get help.

*Fourth*, remember the physical symptoms of depression from chapter 1. If you experience significant changes in your sleeping, eating, and/or crying patterns, and if these symptoms persist for more than a week or so, they should not be ignored.

*Fifth*, listen to your friends. I don't mean listen to all their advice, because surely they will tell you many conflicting things. Friends are usually well-meaning but rarely well-informed. Yet if more than one friend or loved one tells you that you aren't yourself lately, or that you should talk to your pastor or seek professional counsel, it's generally a good indication that things are going to get worse and not better, without help.

## Improving Your Skills

Another, quite legitimate reason for seeking professional counsel is simply when you become dissatisfied with your level of emotional functioning, communicating, or relating.

If you taught yourself how to play tennis, enjoyed the game, and were satisfied with your level of play, there would be no reason to seek professional instruction. But if you started dating someone who competed on the collegiate level, or if you joined a country club, or started playing tennis with your boss, you might become dissatisfied with your skills and want to improve them by going to a professional.

A psychologist is the emotions professional and he gives emotion lessons or communication lessons or even relationship lessons. Depending on the training and background of the psychologist, he or she might even give instruction in arguing or sexual technique. It is best to think of the psychologist as the emotions pro, not someone who heals the emotionally sick, or cares for the crazy.

## Informal Counsel

Once someone has decided to talk about their depression, many prefer to talk first to a well-respected, wise friend, relative, or church member. Others want to talk to their pastor. Any of these could be a fine choice, but the choice should be made consciously, not impulsively. You don't want to share with a blabbermouth or with someone without a track record of emotional stability.

While it is perfectly reasonable to seek informal counsel first, do not rely on it more than a week or two. If your informal counselor is not succeeding in relieving your depression, then he is having trouble uncovering the conflict that's at its source. He may simply not know what to do to help you, or may be giving you wrong advice.

Beware of a counselor who talks too much or preaches at you. Depressions become unclogged by careful listening and detective work. Counselors are supposed to help you find the hidden emotion. They can't do that if they are talking or preaching.

Also, beware of a counselor who is too free with advice and too quick with answers to your questions. Everyone is different, so pat answers are not only often wrong, but unfair to the depressed person. Free advice is generally worth just about what you pay for it. There are, of course, some notable exceptions to this "rule," among them many pastors with an effective counseling ministry.

## Choosing a Therapist

It's unfortunate, but by the time many people have been depressed long enough to admit they need professional treatment, they don't have the energy to do a thorough screening of all the mental health professionals. Too by that time, they may not be thinking very clearly. Thus an important decision is often made under poor circumstances. To try to rectify this problem, here are some guidelines to consider.

*First, a depressed Christian should see a competent Christian therapist whenever possible.* This is such an important issue that the Bible speaks quite specifically about it when it says, "Blessed is the man that walketh *not* in the counsel of the ungodly" (Ps. 1:1, KJV, italics added).

Counseling is an important profession, an important role, and an important ministry. As evidence of that, one of the many names given to Christ, and the first name on one of the lists, is "Wonderful Counselor" (Isa. 9:6). The Lord Jesus is *the* Wonderful Counselor and the Christian counselor is, at best, only a representative of Him. Look for a therapist who is consciously dependent on God's wisdom and healing power. Christ *is* the only really Wonderful Counselor. It only makes sense to go to a counselor who trained under Him, communicates about your situation with Him, and follows His principles with you during therapy.

The other major reason why Christians should seek out Christian therapists is because the Christian's world view is fundamentally different than the non-Christian's world view. If you're going to go to someone to help "straighten you out," doesn't it make sense to go to someone with the same idea of what it means to be "straight" or "healthy"?

Some non-Christian therapists think faith and religion are neurotic, and therefore see religion as the depressed person's problem. While there are certainly some neurotic thoughts about religion, faith in Christ is *not* neurotic, and can and should be an important part of depression's cure. If God made us to be dependent on Him, and I believe He did, then it is not possible to be really "whole" without knowing Christ.

If there are no Christian mental health professionals in your town or within reasonable reach, and no pastors with sufficient mental health background to treat your depression, *choose carefully* from those therapists available. Be sure to tell prospective counselors about your faith and ask how they would deal with it.

It is perfectly appropriate to telephone a psychologist and ask key questions. (By the way, most times psychologists will have to call you back, since they are not interrupted when they are with patients.) You might say, "I am looking for someone to treat my depression but I have a couple of questions I need to ask you. I am an evangelical Christian and my faith is important to me. I don't want to see someone who thinks faith is neurotic or who would encourage me to do anything that would be contrary to my faith. How do you handle this?"

It is also perfectly appropriate to ask a question such as, "I don't mean to be nosy, but do you attend church regularly?" If you ask these two questions of three or four competent mental health professionals, you will probably find that you feel much more comfortable with one of the phone interviewees than with the others. A few other suggestions: When you interview therapists, it's best to write down your questions ahead of time. Don't preach. Don't use "in words" that only other longtime Christians would understand. Don't be defensive about your faith. Do be straightforward, polite, and brief.

## Competence

*If the first thing to look for in a therapist is his faith or reaction to it, the second is his professional competence.* And you can examine competence by two means: reputation and professional credentials.

Let's deal with credentials first. To begin, look at his education. Does this person have a doctorate or a master's degree? Is the doctorate earned or honorary? Is it in psychology or psychiatry, or some closely related field? Ask questions. Everyone is not alike. *All Christians are not competent* and having a title doesn't guarantee adequate training. Would you send your daughter to a surgeon who got his degree from a correspondence school? Of course not. If you wouldn't trust her gall bladder to a quack, why trust her brain and mind to one?

Is this person licensed by the state? If so, what does the license say? If not, why not? (Generally speaking, stay away from non-licensed counselors.) Does he have credentials from professional organizations?

You may rightfully feel that these are too many questions for you to ask in your depressed state. If so, I suggest you write down the questions and ask an assertive friend or relative to get the information for you. If you find a "professional" who gets defensive about this scrutiny, keep looking—he's not your man.

Regarding reputation: Ask the pastors of two or three large churches in your area whom they recommend. Ask your family doctor. If you know a Christian physician, ask his opinion. If the same names keep coming up, you're in good shape. Call the recommended therapists and ask your screening questions. If you know people who have been depressed and received helpful counseling ask them whom they recommend. Or you might know someone who went through successful marriage counseling. That doesn't mean the same counselor is good at handling depression, but it is worth checking out.

## What to Expect in Counseling

Counseling is often a very creative process and no two counselors or two depressed people are exactly alike. Still, you can generally expect the following: First, *you* are going to do most of the talking. You know yourself on the inside better than anyone, and if you'll let yourself talk, you'll end up talking about the important issues. Sure, a counselor will ask questions and make comments from time to time, but he can't say any combination of words to stop your depression. Therapy can be compared to piano lessons. At piano lessons, the student plays and the teacher listens and comments. At emotion lessons, the student talks and the teacher listens and makes comments.

Second, therapy time is structured, i.e., limited. It is almost always the amateur counselor who goes for hour after hour with a patient. The professional knows problems are almost never fixed in one session—they took months or years to create so they won't disappear in an hour. Besides, the professional doesn't conduct marathon therapy sessions with a patient because he has another patient scheduled an hour from now.

Some people are put off by a therapist saying that time is up, but most everyone adjusts to the reality that a session is scheduled to begin at a specific time, go for 45 minutes to an hour, and stop. If you're late, don't be surprised when the session ends as scheduled. Your time starts at the appointed hour and if you're late, it comes out of your time. Of course, if the therapist is late you are still entitled to the full session.

Third, therapy time costs money. If a Christian is a professional piano teacher or plumber, very few people expect "freebies" just because the teacher or plumber is a Christian. God's Word says a laborer is worthy of his hire (Matt. 10:10; 1 Tim. 5:18), and, believe me, it *is* labor to listen to depression and emotional pain for eight hours a day.

If the expense per hour bothers you, it might be better to think of it in terms of the total outlay over, let's say, four to six months. While the cost is expensive, compare it to what you would pay a surgeon to take one hour to remove your gall bladder. Besides, the depression is probably causing you more pain and disruption than the gall bladder ever was. Some people prefer to think of the money as weekly payments on a total fee.

Others take out a loan equal to four to six months of sessions and then make monthly payments to the bank. That way they can spread out the payments.

## Prayer in Counseling

Does a Christian psychologist pray with his counselees? The only answer I know is, "That depends." I pray with a few, but not with most of mine. My reason is primarily that I ended up doing more preaching in the prayer than praying. Also, many of my counselees are not Christians. I do pray *for* all my patients, and I'm in an attitude of prayer *during* the therapy, constantly asking for wisdom, but not usually aloud. As I say, this is a very individual thing, but don't be surprised if it doesn't happen. Of course, if you'd feel more comfortable with prayer, it's OK to ask, but if *you* pray for the session *beforehand* it makes just as much sense.

## Length of Therapy and When to Stop

I'm often asked, "How will I know when I'm ready to stop therapy? Will you tell me or will I need to tell you?" These are good questions. Part of the answer is found in the emotions pro—tennis pro analogy I used earlier. You stop lessons when you are satisfied with your new level of competence.

One factor which compounds this simple answer is that it takes a much shorter time to cure the symptom than it does to achieve a higher level of functioning to avoid repeating the same mistakes and descending into another depression.

As you can see in figure 11-1 on page 116, phase one of therapy may last a rather short period of time, as little as two to three months in some cases. Phase one is removing the symptom, helping unclog the emotional blockage, and relieving the depression.

Phase two takes longer and the rate of improving your level of functioning is not as rapid as in phase one. But as figure 11-1

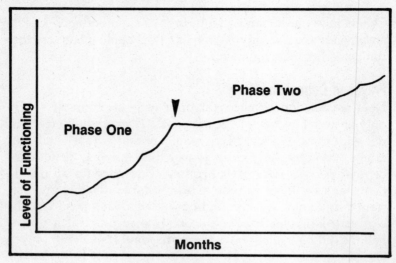

FIGURE 11-1

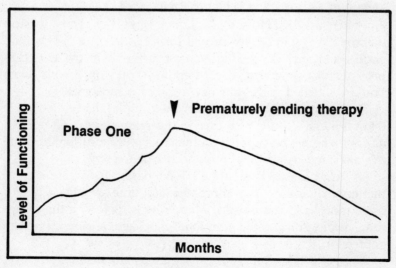

FIGURE 11-2

shows, there is significant improvement nonetheless.

While anyone has the right to stop therapy when he feels better, as we see in figure 11-2 on page 116, if you stop too soon, you are in danger of repeating old mistakes and suffering another depression. When it is time to stop therapy, the therapist and the counselee usually agree.

# 12

## How You Can Help Others

"Keith, I don't want to intrude, but I wanted to talk to you because, frankly, I'm concerned about you. You haven't seemed yourself for the last several weeks. You seem depressed. I just want to say I've noticed. If you want to talk or need help or anything, let me know. Or if you'd rather I mind my own business, that's OK too."

The preceding paragraph illustrates one person caring enough about another to take a risk. It happens, but it needs to happen much, much more.

Depression often begins so gradually that the depressed person is not totally aware of what is happening. He doesn't realize how differently he looks and acts. Close friends and family often notice first, and if they know what to do and are willing to become involved, they can help prevent major emotional difficulty.

### Good Listening
The biggest mistake the nonprofessional counselor is likely to make is to talk too much. Imagine this dialogue:

JEFF: So, Tim, tell me what's bothering you. I mean just go ahead and talk about it.

TIM: Well, I . . .

JEFF: That's good. Just open up and share what's on your heart, brother. You know I'm here to help.

TIM: Well, I've been feeling a bit down lately and I . . .

JEFF: Yep, I knew you were down. You know, two weeks ago at the Sunday School dinner, what was that two or three weeks ago? Well, anyway, I was saying to Martha, "You know Tim just doesn't seem himself lately. I think he must be feeling down about something." But you know, I was down about four or five years ago when we got that new mortgage. Man, I was really worried about that but after a while things got better. You know?

That may be an extreme example, but it demonstrates that overwhelming the conversation isn't at all helpful because the depressed person is the one who needs to do the talking. Unfortunately, amateur counselors often naively think that by their own example they can point *the way* to someone. In the process, they come across as rather self-centered.

It's also somewhat self-centered to think we have more answers, more wisdom, more ideas, or more common sense than a depressed person. Depressed people are often talked down to as though they are mentally retarded—and that is a mistake.

## Don't Fix It!

Certainly the biggest misunderstanding the nonprofessional counselor has about his role is a tendency to see himself as the "fix-it man"—solving the depressed person's emotional problems.

Probably the broadest group of people who misunderstand this principle is husbands. When wives share negative feelings about their day, or their job, or the children, many husbands feel that they are supposed to "fix it" by telling them what to do (when really just a listening ear will suffice). The end result is predictable. Either the husbands become irritated because they don't know what advice to give (and thus feel somewhat pressured). Or they become angry because their wives don't or won't follow their advice.

If you are counseling a depressed person, relax. There is no need to feel responsible for fixing his problem. The responsibility is his alone. Your sole purpose is to support and accompany him on his trip, while perhaps pointing out observations about his emotions along the way. The depressed person is "retarded" only in one area, and that is in the emotional conflict that has been repressed rather than expressed. The counselor guides him back through his emotional maze to look for logjams. But even when the counselor is quite sure he knows what emotion has been repressed, he only guides the depressed person through that situation and suggests something like, "I wonder if that made you angry." In this way the depressed person discovers his own emotions.

I have generally found that if I say more than two or three sentences in a row even counselees who have driven a considerable distance and are paying a significant amount of money to talk with me will tune me right out. Their eyes glaze over. They are too involved in their own pain to hear much that I might say. I must only make brief suggestions.

## Understanding

I can just hear someone asking, "If they don't want me to fix anything, why are these people talking to me? What do they want from me?" Well, I'm glad you asked. There are two very specific things that upset people want from their counselors—whether the counselor be a husband or wife, a friend, or a professional—the first is understanding, the second is caring.

Understanding is simply letting the depressed person know that you have some idea what it must be like for him or what he must be feeling.

Darlene, a sweet gal who worked as a bank teller, was emotionally sensitive. When she had difficulty balancing her accounts at the end of a day, she would begin to get nervous. The more nervous she became, the less accurate she was. To make matters worse, her branch manager was harsh and demanding and used language Darlene had never before had directed at her. The more her boss yelled, the more upset Darlene became. By the time she arrived home in the evening, Darlene was emotionally exhausted.

Darlene's husband Dick asked my advice. "Darlene was crying about her job again last night, and about her boss yelling at her. I told her what she should do about it and why she didn't have to let that bother her, but it doesn't seem to help. She says that I don't understand her. It seems like the same thing happens at least once a week. What in the world does she want me to say?"

Dick's question is common. Frankly, I doubt if any of us have been exempt from the frustration of trying to help our friends, our spouse, or our children in hurting times. We try to help them feel better, but they don't listen to us or take our advice. When we've done everything we know to do, they still don't feel any better. Why?

## Doers and Be-ers

When something is broken, we don't generally spend a lot of time thinking about what it feels like to be broken. When something is broken, we usually try to fix it.

At least half the world thinks this way. (I'm one of them.) We are called "doers." Doers are the ones most likely to be frustrated when trying to counsel friends or relatives because the skill needed for effective counseling is not a "doing" skill but a "being" skill. We need to *be* understanding.

Because men tend to be doers and women tend to be be-ers, we'll use a husband and wife relationship to illustrate (the husband in the counseling role and the wife in the role of the person who is upset). Remember though, if a husband is upset, he still needs the same understanding that a wife needs.

Nancy and John had planned a romantic Saturday afternoon picnic, but when she saw that the sky was getting cloudy, she asked, "What will we do if it rains?"

John's first impulse was to say, "If it rains, we'll go inside or get wet." But fortunately, he had been counseled how to properly respond to his wife's needs, and remembered that his instinct was to respond on a doing level, rather than on a level which understands emotions (a being level).

With some thought, John realized that Nancy was trying to convey her worried feeling that the happy, peaceful time she was hoping to experience had been threatened by the weather. Knowing this, John was able to respond to his wife's emotions rather than her words, "Honey, even if we have to have our picnic in the kitchen, it's just being with you that really makes me happy." Learning how to do this is probably the single most important skill for counseling one another.

## What Your Friend Wants

An upset friend wants something from you that is really quite alien to your basic performance-oriented nature. She wants you to understand and care about what she's feeling. If she is lonely, you are not meeting her needs by telling her to meet people. Her need is to know that *you* know she feels lonely, to know that you have some idea about how she must feel, and that you're sorry she feels bad.

When you tell your children, "Sorry doesn't get the garbage taken out," you don't want them to talk about it, you want action. When your friend is upset, she is exactly the opposite. She doesn't want action. She wants to talk about it.

As I stated earlier, two basic principles can be applied when your friends or loved ones are upset. When used properly, these principles will help you communicate the love and concern that you have for them in a way they will understand and in a way that will meet their needs.

Your friend needs you to understand her emotions. Therefore, the first principle is to tell her what you think she is feeling. The best way to know what she's feeling is to imagine yourself in her situation. This is not the same thing as telling her what you would have done in her circumstance (which is *not* what she needs).

Liz came home from the store in tears. "I'll never go back there again. I could have just died."

"What happened?" asked her husband Fred.

"I wrote a check to pay for the children's clothes and when the girl saw my name on the check she called the manager. My name was on a list of people not to accept checks from. The manager came out and all these people were standing in line while he told me I had written two bad checks in his store. Then I said, 'No way was that me' and I started to cry. Finally he took me to his office to show me the checks. They were written with the same name as mine, but she has a different middle name and an 'e' in her last name. Then he was all apologies, but we were in his office and nobody heard him apologize to me. After that, he went out and yelled at the cashier. I'm never going back there!"

If you were Fred, how would you respond to meet Liz's needs in this situation?

 a. Say it was just a mistake. It could happen to anybody. Don't worry about it.
 b. Get mad and go see the manager.
 c. Call a lawyer.
 d. Tell her what she should have done.
 e. Tell her God had a purpose in it.

f. None of the above.

The correct answer is "f," none of the above, because more than anything, she wants understanding and these don't communicate understanding to her.

Here are some other possible responses:

a. Oh! That must have been awful.

b. You must have felt like going through the floor.

c. I'll bet you felt like punching somebody.

Any of these responses would have been good, because in each of them, Fred is telling Liz what he thinks she was feeling.

## Caring

The second principle is, that in addition to telling her what you think she's feeling, you can tell her how *you* feel about what she's feeling. Add your own caring feelings to your statements about her feelings in the preceding examples and you will add depth and warmth to your responses.

a. Oh! That must have been awful.

I'm so sorry that it happened.

b. You must have felt like going through the floor.

I wish I could have been there with you.

c. I'll bet you felt like punching somebody.

I certainly don't blame you.

When you don't know what to say, a pure caring response — "Oh, I'm so sorry that happened"—is generally best.

Tell an upset or depressed person how you feel about what he's feeling *only* when what you feel is positive. If you think that his feeling is dumb, don't say it! Just stick to telling him what you think he is feeling until you *do* feel something positive.

## Understanding Your Children

The principles given for understanding friends or spouses apply equally to handling children. Here are some examples:

"Oh, that must really hurt. Mommy's sorry that happened."
"It's hard to lose, isn't it?"
"It hurts when friends don't act like friends, doesn't it?"
"I'm sorry Don broke your date. I know how that must hurt."

Tell a child what you think he is feeling and tell him how you feel about his feeling. It's particularly important that you get young children to talk about their hurts and that you suggest a label for their feelings. They may not have an abstract vocabulary adequate enough to express, or even to know exactly what they are feeling. All they may know is that it feels very bad all over. By helping them find words that specifically label their pain, you give them limits to the hurt. This helps them realize that it is not the whole world that has gone against them, just a certain situation or person. If they have a label for their feelings, they can handle them much better.

You may have heard your child say such general, all-inclusive statements as, "Oh, I can never do anything right," or, "Everybody hates me." If you can help him figure out exactly what is bothering him, he will feel a lot better than a generalized "everything is rotten."

So the next time you see your child become greatly upset while trying to learn how to ride a bicycle or after striking out three times in a row, try to come up with an understanding and caring label-response for his feelings. For example: "It's disappointing when you don't learn things as quickly as you would like, isn't it?" or, "It makes you mad when you don't do things perfectly the first time, doesn't it?"

## Responses to Avoid

Don't try to communicate instructions to hurting persons. Trying to teach at that time only communicates a lack of concern on your part. Since you *are* concerned, you need to show it in a way that will be understood. Avoid making comments like:

"Now, why did you do that?"

"Won't you ever learn?"

"I told you to be careful."

Also avoid trying to convince, convict, or argue. If you do that, you are trying to move depressed persons from where *they are* to where *you are* without communicating to them that you really care about where they are. In short, you are focusing on your own point of view, and that's not an effective way to practice the understanding and caring response.

Avoid preaching and condemning. Stay away from even implying messages like, "That's a dumb feeling," or "You shouldn't feel that way." If depressed persons feel a certain way, then that's where they are, and telling them not to be there doesn't change a thing. Even if their feeling really is wrong, they will have to look at it honestly and feel your personal support before they can let go of it.

In summary, we need to be aware of our tendency to focus on behavior and try to avoid a response to behavior patterns only. We can show our understanding by focusing on a person's emotional condition and sharing with him what we think he is feeling.

## Prayer

It's difficult to imagine a successful Christian counselor who is not involved in prayer. Whether you are doing formal or informal counseling, whether professional or amateur, whether with a church member or a spouse, a friend or a stranger, you *must* pray to be an effective Christian counselor.

We need to pray for wisdom, discernment, and direction. God's Word says that He gives wisdom generously to those who ask (James 1:5). It is both foolish and egotistical to think that we know what changes another of God's children should make in his life, without prayerfully seeking God's direction.

Intercessory prayer is also important; that is, we need to pray throughout the week for the needs, protection, spiritual growth, and health of that person we are counseling.

Finally, while you are actually counseling an individual you also need an attitude of prayerful dependence on God. To keep this attitude consciously present at all times is fighting against the flesh, the old nature which urges you to depend on yourself. In other words, you won't always succeed, but don't stop trying.

Whether you actually pray aloud with the person you are counseling depends both on you and on the situation. Obviously, when your husband or wife comes home upset, he or she wants you to care, to understand, and to listen. Interrupting to say, "Let's pray about it," is usually not well received.

## Bible Reading

Bible reading in a counseling situation is sometimes beneficial, sometimes not. Just remember that the need to communicate understanding and caring is usually much more important in counseling than the need to communicate facts (even biblical facts).

Bible reading for the Christian who counsels is *absolutely essential*. It is sword practice readying you for battle. Christ prayed that his followers would be made holy (sanctified) through the Word (John 17:17). Knowing the Bible and being able to quote it are important elements in being able to resist Satan's temptations. Plus, the principles found in the Bible *are* principles for living. The Bible has been called the owner's operating manual for the believer. If we are to help straighten people out, we must remember the definition of "straight" is found in God's Word.

Having said all this, too much Bible quoting in a counseling situation, even a very informal, one-time session, usually makes people feel worse (i.e., condemned or misunderstood), not better. A counselor who uses (or misuses) the Bible by listing dozens of verses to support his case is *not* counseling by understanding and caring, but instead is trying to move a person from point A to point B (whether he wants to go or not).

Unless we remember that most depression is caused by an emotional logjam that needs to become unclogged by finding the hidden emotion, we are susceptible to the temptation of lecturing or preaching instead of listening and caring.

## Conclusion

I want to encourage people to be nonjudgmental when a Christian friend or loved one is depressed. As we have seen, while there can be a spiritual component to depression, depression is generally an emotional condition rather than a spiritual one. Despite their good motives, many (if not most) depressed Christians become depressed because they repress emotional expression. As we love and understand one another, we create an atmosphere in which people who are upset can feel free to *talk about* their feelings, rather than hold them in. Our love and acceptance, therefore, can help to prevent or cure a multitude of depressions.